It is an honor to know Luann and [...]  alk with her through parts of this jou[...] his book was gained. There is a vast tre[...] ho are "drowning" and may feel unabl[...] et time of prayer with Luann crying o[...] ly healed. This book is fulfillment of t[...] n total wholeness or you desire to com[...] guide or others to help them reach their full potential, this book is a "must read." Thank you, Luann, for fighting through the battle, for taking the time to capture the wisdom learned, and for putting it into book form so that others can walk in wholeness.

—Pastor Verna Lilley
Daughter of God, Pastor's Wife, Mother, Friend
First Assembly of God, Waterbury, CT

As a pastoral counselor, I have seen the connection between emotional and physical health. In *Holy Spirit Psychology*, Luann pens out how to recognize toxic emotions that may be at the very root of the problems in your life, keeping you bound from experiencing freedom, health, and healing. Luann shares from her own life experiences and the journey that led to her own freedom and healing, which has produced in her a passion to help others receive emotional and physical healing. What I like about this book is that it is a practical, informative guide that gives you the *"how to"* meant to help the reader on their personal journey to wholeness. Luann leads you from toxicity to wholeness. I highly recommend this book if you are serious about walking in true freedom and wholeness. If you are a pastoral counselor, clinician, or doctor, this is a must read!

—Carmela Muratori
Cofounder, Calvary Life Family Worship Center
Certified Pastoral Counselor

Holy Spirit Psychology is a refreshing change from the humanistic approach to wholeness. With solid scientific evidence, Luann shows you how the Holy Spirit brings real wholeness to your body, soul, and spirit. This book can help you get to the root of your issues and will help you to go deeper in your relationship with Jesus. If you are living a life that is limited and controlled by fear, you need this book. If you are living with chronic illness or pain with no known cause, you need this book. Luann is a living example of how God uses our trials and tribulations to equip and prepare us to minister to others. *Holy Spirit Psychology* will help you to experience freedom in Christ and live a life that brings glory to God.

REV. SHARON B. FRANKEL
ORDAINED MINISTER
ASSEMBLIES OF GOD SOUTHERN NEW ENGLAND MINISTRY NETWORK

Holy Spirit Psychology

Recover Your Emotional and Physical Health

Luann Dunnuck

CREATION HOUSE

HOLY SPIRIT PSYCHOLOGY: RECOVER YOUR EMOTIONAL AND PHYSICAL
HEALTH by Luann Dunnuck
Published by Creation House
A Charisma Media Company
600 Rinehart Road
Lake Mary, Florida 32746
www.charismamedia.com

This book or parts thereof may not be reproduced in any form, stored in a retrieval system, or transmitted in any form by any means—electronic, mechanical, photocopy, recording, or otherwise—without prior written permission of the publisher, except as provided by United States of America copyright law.

Unless otherwise noted, all Scripture quotations are from the New King James Version of the Bible. Copyright © 1979, 1980, 1982 by Thomas Nelson, Inc., publishers. Used by permission.

Scripture quotations marked AMP are from the Amplified Bible. Old Testament copyright © 1965, 1987 by the Zondervan Corporation. The Amplified New Testament copyright © 1954, 1958, 1987 by the Lockman Foundation. Used by permission.

Scripture quotations marked KJV are from the King James Version of the Bible.

Scripture quotations marked NAS are from the New American Standard Bible–Updated Edition, Copyright © 1960, 1962, 1963, 1968, 1971, 1972, 1973, 1975, 1977, 1995 by The Lockman Foundation. Used by permission. (www.Lockman.org)

Scripture quotations marked TLB are from The Living Bible. Copyright © 1971. Used by permission of Tyndale House Publishers, Inc., Wheaton, IL 60189. All rights reserved.

English definitions are from *Merriam-Webster OnLine*, http://www.merriam-webster.com/, or the *Encarta World English Dictionary* (Microsoft Corp, 2000).

Greek and Hebrew definitions are derived from *Strong's Exhaustive Concordance of the Bible*, ed. James Strong, Nashville, TN: Thomas Nelson Publishers, 1997.

The companion workbook is available at www.luanndunnuck.com.

Design Director: Justin Evans
Cover design by Terry Clifton

Copyright © 2014 by Luann Dunnuck
All rights reserved.

Visit the author's website: http://www.luanndunnuck.com.

Library of Congress CataloginginPublication Data: 2014953364
International Standard Book Number: 978-1-62998-397-4
E-book International Standard Book Number: 978-1-62998-397-4

While the author has made every effort to provide accurate telephone numbers and Internet addresses at the time of publication, neither the publisher nor the author assumes any responsibility for errors or for changes that occur after publication.

First edition

14 15 16 17 18 — 987654321
Printed in the United States of America

This book is dedicated to the reader, to the person who is discouraged and frustrated, to the one who has almost given up hope and faith. Change is on the horizon. It is my prayer that you will find redemption and transformation in the area of your struggle. It's through the kindness of God that we are restored to wholeness.

Contents

Introduction ix

PART 1:
FOUNDATIONAL TRUTHS

1 When Nothing Is Working 1
2 The Principal of Agreement 12
3 Origins of Negative Thoughts 18

PART 2:
CAUSE AND REPAIR OF DAMAGED EMOTIONS

4 Stress 29
5 Broken Heart 43
6 Self-Reproach 51
7 Guilt and Accusation 68
8 Worry, Anxiety, and Fear 82
9 Depression 102
10 Anger and Bitterness 112
11 Unforgiveness 127

PART 3:
CONTINUING TO OVERCOME

12 Your Relationship with God 145
13 A New Door 145
14 Collection of Prayers 162

Notes 169
About the Author 175
Contact the Author 176
Companion Workbook 177
Other Books by the Author 178

INTRODUCTION

I BELIEVE THIS BOOK is going to bring healing to your mind, body, and your spirit. Before you begin this journey of healing, I want to briefly share with you how to use this book to receive the most benefit from it. There are three components to receive healing from the damaged emotions that plague us.

1. **Identify the root or the why behind your struggle with that emotion.** As you read the chapter on the emotion you struggle with and answer questions from the corresponding workbook (available at www.luanndunnuck.com), I believe the Holy Spirit will show you the "why" behind your struggle. It's important to know why, because you cannot fix a problem that you cannot identify. The Holy Spirit is the best Counselor, Wisdom giver, and Comforter. Once you identify the root, it's on to the second component of your healing.

2. **Pull the root out.** Okay, so you may be asking how do you pull the root of trauma or hurt out of your soul. Once the root is identified, talk about it, journal about it, cry over it, and talk to God about it *until the hurt, disappointment or even shock of it fades.* This is healing. When the wound no longer grips your soul, there is a level of healing. The memory will be there, but the sting of the memory should no longer torment you. This process may happen as you initially share the trauma, or it may require longer term Christian counseling. After you have gone through this process, then you pray and release it to God. There will be a prayer at the end of each chapter that will allow you to cast your trauma on the cross of Jesus Christ. The cross of Jesus provides healing for us on many levels. It's also important to say the prayer out loud. Your brain believes what it hears coming out of your mouth.

3. **The mental stop sign.** Once you have exposed the root or the why behind your struggle and you have released it to God, understand that the enemy of your soul—the devil—will try again to tempt

you to fall victim to that negative emotion. For example; if you struggle with a root of rejection because an important person in your life abandoned you, understand that the enemy may try and come back with negative thoughts about how *you are still* unlovable, not valuable, worthless, etc. This is where it is a must that we hold up that mental stop sign and say no! No! I *will not* come under the influence of that toxic emotion again. I refuse to come into agreement with that toxic emotion. The more you do this, the easier it becomes. Eventually you will feel how freeing it is to live without spiraling down into that emotion. You will quickly recognize when that old way of negative thinking tries to come back. It's like living without that that monkey on your back. When that monkey tries to climb back on your back, you will recognize its heavy weight and command it to leave. It's the same way with negative emotions. When you learn to change your thinking for the better, you begin to lead the abundant life that Jesus desires to give you and you no longer are comfortable with that monkey on your back.

It is important to note that if someone struggles with one negative emotion they may also struggle with another negative emotion. Our negative thinking is entwined. For example; if someone struggles panic attacks, this may be the result of a broken heart. Or, if someone struggles with depression, they may have a root of self-rejection. It is essential that all the chapters are read and reflected upon to understand why we have difficulty in a certain area.

There is a companion workbook to this book (available at www.luanndunnuck.com). The function of the workbook is to ask questions that will inspire you to get to the root of the issue. The best way to use the workbook is to read a chapter in this book and then answer the workbook questions on the same negative emotion. For example after you finish reading the chapter in this book on fear, then go to the workbook and answer the corresponding questions on fear. The two are designed to identify the origin of the toxic emotion and then to bring the root cause out to the surface and into the light so that you can heal from it and then subsequently heal from the toxic emotion.

I have used the above method and had much success. But there were also times of acute distress when I sought out Christian counseling. I in no way put down conventional counseling. In fact, there are times when we may benefit greatly from a Christian counselor. My only objection is when counseling becomes a way of life and we continue to go around the same mountain for decades. This is when I would suggest that we need to get to the root of the issue.

The CDC has said that 80 percent of all illness has a "stressor" behind it.[1] If we could take away the stressor, or the root of our negative thinking, then our body could heal. You will learn in many of these chapters that how we feel physically is related to what's going on in our thinking. I would always encourage you to follow the advice of your physician, psychiatrist, psychologist, or counselor. I believe God uses medicine when we need it and a compassionate counselor when we need it.

Are You Ready?

Are you ready to discover the freedom that is available to you? Are you ready to begin a journey to free your damaged emotions? As you read through this book, allow the Holy Spirit to show you truths that will accomplish freedom from your emotional and physical afflictions. The Bible refers to the Holy Spirit as our "Counselor" (John 14:26, AMP) The Holy Spirit knows the deep issues in your soul, and He knows how to unlock the pain in your heart.

In addition, this book is also designed to be a timely reference when going through a difficult season. For example, long after you have read this book you may go through an experience with long-term stress, anger, worry, unforgiveness, or any other negative emotion. You can reread the specific chapter that covers the issue you are facing to gain insights as to how to deal with that specific struggle. I have found it helpful to revisit certain truths when I am confronted with difficult situations.

I know what it's like to live for decades with a variety of toxic emotions and become sick because of it. I also know what it's like to look back and see how far you've come. Several times God says in the Bible that there is nothing too hard for Him. If you think your situation or your affliction is too difficult for God, I would answer that by the Word of God found in the Bible:

> Ah, Lord God! Behold, You have made the heavens and the earth by Your great power and outstretched arm. There is nothing too hard for You.
> —Jeremiah 32:17

> Behold, I am the Lord, the God of all flesh. Is there anything too hard for Me?
> —Jeremiah 32:27

There is no bondage, no affliction, nor human condition that is too hard for our all powerful, loving God. May God bless your mind, body, and spirit as turn the pages of this book!

Part 1

FOUNDATIONAL TRUTHS

Chapter 1
WHEN NOTHING IS WORKING

What do you do when you have prayed and prayed and had others pray, yet you see no change? What do you do when you've been to many doctors and followed everything they asked you to do, yet you see no change. This is the place I was at during a very serious illness. I was at my wits end.

I understand the utter frustration and discouragement that comes from emotional and physical afflictions. I recognize the defeat someone can feel when *nothing is working*. I felt completely devastated with my condition; and at times I even dreaded waking up in the morning, because I knew that pain and sickness would be waiting for me. I was out of options and just about out of hope. I faced years of panic attacks that were the result of a broken heart. I know what it's like to suffer physically, and I am well acquainted with emotional suffering. If you are in a place of emotional or physical suffering, you have the right book in your hand.

WHERE ARE YOU GOD?

When we face trials of emotional or physical sickness, it's easy to ask the question: "Where are you God?" I asked this question many times. I would bombard heaven with pleas for instant healing; and when healing didn't come, I went on a quest to learn why. It was at this point that I studied the Gospels and read how Jesus ministered to the sick. I read testimonies of people who received healing. I researched blocks to healing and generational curses. I studied anything I could get my hands on that would teach me about emotional and physical healing. My conclusion was this: when healing does not happen right away, it's because God wants to heal us at a deeper level, at the root cause of our pain.

"Where are you God?" became my frequently asked question. I *perceived* that God would not help me. I said to God, "Create in me a clean heart and get rid of the junk in me that is keeping me sick." If God were to instantaneously heal us, we perhaps would not be motivated to clean up the junk of our lives. And if we don't clean up the mess of our lives, the sickness can potentially come right back. Many times the sickness is a fruit of a deeper root in our life. God is after the root; and when He pulls the root out from our lives the sickness dries up.

It took time for me to learn this principle. I had to sift through disappointments to find hope that I could be healthy and strong again. I remember sitting in the waiting room of my doctor's office watching the "healthy people" buzz by me. I would say to myself, "I hope I will be able to have the strength to move around like that again." And I do!

When I was sick and housebound, I remember lying on one of my couches that had a view of a large tree in our front yard. I watched the tree change from the summer's bright green leaves to the beautiful autumn colors of fall, to being snow-covered white, back to spring's budding blossoms. And then I watched it all over again. It was during that time that I agonized over losing my health, I felt stuck in a house on a couch. I grieved over not being able to go on with my life. Self-pity was my close friend and loneliness was its cousin. I would admire those around me who could move about.

If I could go back and give myself advice during this time, I would remind myself of four words that have gotten countless people through difficulties: This too shall pass. What I didn't know is that it's in difficulties that our faith grows deep in God and our relationship with God soars to a new glorious level. If we can hang on long enough, we will find that our difficulty will pass. God admonishes us to stay focused on His goodness.

Philippians 4:8 tells us to think on things that are of a good report:

> Finally, brethren, whatever things are true, whatever things are noble, whatever things are just, whatever things are pure, whatever things are lovely, whatever things are of *good report*, if there is any virtue and if there is anything praiseworthy—meditate on these things.
>
> —Philippians 4:8, emphasis added

The Battle of Trust

During the trying months and years of sickness, I remember saying to God on many occasions, "Why are You allowing me to suffer like this? If You love me so much, why aren't You helping me?" I was saying the same thing Jesus said to His father on the cross, "My God, My God, why have You forsaken Me?" (Matt. 27:46). I was saying the same thing Mary said to Jesus when her brother Lazarus died, "Lord, if You had been here, my brother would not have died" (John 11:32). I was saying the same thing the prophet Jeremiah said to God, "Woe is me, my mother, That you have borne me" (Jer. 15:10). Jeremiah felt rejected and wondered why he was even born. So, you see you are in good company if you have ever asked God why. If you are carrying any guilt over asking God why, let it go. God is big enough to handle our guilt.

Let's examine Mary, the sister of Lazarus for a moment. This is the same Mary who sat at Jesus' feet and anointed his feet for burial with her hair (John 11:2). Mary was a worshipper of God. John 11:3 says, "The sisters sent to Him [Jesus] saying, 'Lord, behold, he [Lazarus] whom you love is sick." Mary, Martha, and their brother, Lazarus, were close with Jesus. Jesus had a familiar relationship with the family. The text tells us that Mary and Martha called for Jesus to come to their home because Lazarus was sick (v. 5). The Bible tells us that Jesus waited two more days after hearing their request before heading to their house (v. 6). Jesus appears to be in no hurry to heal Lazarus.

When Jesus finally gets to the home of Lazarus, he discovers Lazarus "had already been in the tomb for four days" (v. 17). Mary is devastated and greatly disappointed. Mary says to Jesus, "*If* You had been here, my brother would not have died" (v. 32, emphasis added). She is saying to Jesus, "You could have been here to heal my brother, but You weren't. You have the power to heal him, but You didn't." We hear the anguish in Mary's words: "Lord, You could have done something, but You did not."

Have you ever felt like that? Through bitter tears I have said the same thing to God. I have gone so far as to say to God, "You must really hate me to leave me like this." How very sad that I would misinterpret a sickness for God's disdain of me. My story, like Mary's story, gets a lot better.

The Bible goes on to tell us that she was weeping, and the others around her were weeping (v. 33a). When Jesus saw the brokenness of the people and how they were in such despair, the Bible tells us that "He groaned in the spirit and was troubled" (v. 33b). Picture Jesus saddened and moved with compassion because of the grief He saw in the people.

That's how Jesus is with you and me. His heart breaks at our pain and our misunderstanding of His ways. We can clearly see the heart of God in this text; God is moved with compassion when He sees your suffering. This was very healing for me—to know that God does not desire that I be stuck in any kind of sickness. Many times He allows the momentary pain to bring about an even greater healing. The following are tender compassionate words from God to us.

> See, I have inscribed you on the palms of My hands.
> —Isaiah 49:16

> As one whom his mother comforts, so I will comfort you.
> —Isaiah 66:13

> I am God, and not man...And I will not come with terror.
> —Hosea 11:9

I had strong misconceptions of who God is and how He saw me. I didn't understand God's love for me then, and I certainly didn't trust Him to heal me. What Mary didn't know and what we do not know, is that the reason God does not step in and fix the situation immediately is because He has an even *greater miracle in mind*. Do we want to live an ordinary life or do we want to be positioned for an extraordinary miracle. Jesus could have come and healed Lazarus, as was common in Jesus' ministry, but Jesus had an even greater miracle to perform—a miracle that would reap far greater dividends: to perform the miracle was that Lazarus was raised from the dead!

There is a principle at work in these verses: the more intense the problem, the more awesome the miracle. Just when we think there is no way out, God is waiting to perform an even greater miracle in our lives. The miracle may not come as we think it should; but nonetheless, let's trust God's miracle power to make us whole—body, soul, and spirit.

Mary's Lesson

Many times I have identified with Mary because all Mary saw was her present suffering, not realizing that Jesus was getting ready to raise her brother from the dead. Jesus was about to do exceeding abundantly above all she could have asked or thought (Eph. 3:20). It's this scripture that I have turned to find comfort in my disappointments. It's this portion of scripture that encouraged me when the sky above me turned grey. This scripture has taught me to wait because God has something better.

We have all been in those seasons of life, when our rainbow of dreams seems to be colorless. It's in these moments that we need to pay close attention to how our heavenly Father is working all things out for our good (Rom. 8:28). You see, in order for our lives to resurrect into a new beginning, there has to be a death of our old routines of thought and behavior. This can be a painful process but a necessary one.

Many years ago I remember listening to Dr. Dobson's "Focus on the Family" program. He recounted how a father had to take his son to the ear doctor for a necessary medical procedure. The son began to scream, "Daddy, please don't let them do this to me! Daddy, please!" The wise father had to help restrain the son for the doctor to do his work. It greatly broke the father's heart that the son could not understand the medical necessity of the procedure. The father knew that if he didn't allow this procedure to be done, his son's future would hold even greater suffering. When I heard this account of the boy's predicament, it helped me understand *why* God allows some situations. I'm not here to debate theology on the question of suffering nor am I trying to explain the ways of God. What I am saying is that there are times God allows the problem to perform a surgery on our soul that will make our life better than it was before.

A JOB SEASON, A JOB REWARD

One leader in my church told me, "You are going through a Job season." No offense to Job, but of all the people in the Bible to identify with, Job was not at the top of my list. Most of you know the story of Job. He lost everything—his children were killed, he was struck with illness, his fortune was lost, and his friends turned against him. The Book of Job goes through the process of Job truly learning who God is and who Job is not. The last chapter of Job tells us that "the LORD blessed the latter days of Job more than his beginning" (Job 42:12).

Think about that statement for a moment. God wants to make us better off than we were before. God is good. I didn't know that deep down, I really didn't believe that God is good. I had a difficult time trusting that God only had my good in mind. In my heart I figured God would not come through for me because others in the past had not come through for me. I felt like I did not really deserve God's goodness. So for me to trust that God would bless my latter days more than my beginning was indeed a process.

I remember a time when the panic attacks were so severe that going out in public places, such as the grocery store or church, was extremely difficult. When I was physically sick, I remember how difficult it was to walk or even think. I was unsure if I had the strength to hold myself up and the energy to get around the house. I would constantly and very tenderly ask God, "You got me God?" And He would gently whisper, "I've got you." I would ask again, "You got me God?" And again He would say, "I've got you." I would ask this over and over again until I felt confident that He literally was holding me up. *I learned I could trust Him.*

When we think about Job and how he persevered in his difficulties, we understand that God did not change Job's situation immediately. I have been in that same dilemma. I asked God to change my circumstances but nothing changed. When I find myself in this dilemma, I know God is desiring to do a deeper work in my soul. This is when I climb up on the heavenly operating table and pray to God that He will remove the impurities from heart so that I can be healed, echoing what King David said, "Create in me a clean heart" (Ps. 51:10). This is a courageous and yet humble prayer to pray. This type of prayer has the potential to reap a healthy body, soul, and spirit.

The story of the little boy with the ear problem can be a picture of God cleaning us up. God puts us on His operating table and removes the impurities and debris that could potentially ruin us. All the while we are screaming, "God, stop! This hurts too much! I can't bear this!" But just like the father who had the resolve to restrain his son, God gently removes the infections of our lives. Just like He did with Job, our loving God is making us better off than we were before.

God restored to Job all that he lost. Not only was Job restored, but the Bible tells us:

> After this Job lived one hundred and forty years, and saw his children and grandchildren for four generations. So Job died, old and full of days.
> —Job 42:16–17

Job lived a long, satisfying life surrounded by family and friends and financial abundance. Yes, he suffered greatly; but when his trial *was over* God blessed Job. Notice I said *when his trial was over*. That is the hope that I want you to keep in your heart: *the trial will be over*.

I remember days when getting out of bed and simply brushing my teeth was an accomplishment. I remember being unable to do simple tasks like cooking a meal or doing laundry. It was during these difficult times that I would remind myself that this too shall pass. And it did!

On a funny note, there were a few times during my sickest days that I would be reminded of the theme song from the movie 1977 *Rocky*, "Gonna Fly Now," composed by Bill Conti with lyrics by Carol Conners and Ayn Robbins. In the scene when Sylvester Stallone is running up the steps in downtown Philadelphia and because of all his training he has gotten stronger and stronger, the theme song is playing in the background: "Trying hard now…Getting strong now…Gonna fly now." While I was waiting for my healing, the theme song to *Rocky* would play in my head. It was a source of encouragement while I was in process of healing.

Sick for a Second Time

I was thirty-nine years old, and for the *second* time in my life I was diagnosed with the same debilitating illness that kept me housebound for almost a year. Why did the sickness come back for a second time? Why did I recover from the illness once before only to have it return even stronger? Here's the answer: God is more interested in healing the emotional pain and ungodly thinking that can *lead* to sickness then just healing our surface problems. God is not interested in a momentary healing when He knows that sickness will come right back if we are not healed on a deeper level. He's not going to put a temporary Band-Aid on our wounds. God, in His wisdom, knows that if your soul gets healed *first* then your body will follow. Why would a loving God heal the body without healing the soul, when perhaps the reason for the sickness in the body is a broken soul? In God's own Word He says, "Beloved, I pray that you may prosper in all things and be in *health*, just as your *soul prospers*" (3 John 1:2, emphasis added). If your soul's not prospering, there is a good chance that your body's not prospering.

Eighty to ninety percent of sickness has a spiritual root behind it.[1] What I mean by spiritual root is that behind many illnesses you may find long-term stress, emotional or physical abuse, negative thinking, unforgiveness, bitterness, rejection, fear, guilt, and the like. All of these topics are covered in the following chapters of this book. It's time we deal with what's really bothering us so we can move forward with our lives and be free from emotional and physical bondages.

Before we go any further, I want to make an important point regarding the above statistic. Even if you're not good in math you can figure out that 80 percent to 90 percent is not 100 percent. This leaves 10 percent to 20 percent of sicknesses that are the result of natural causes, injuries, etc. So I am not advocating that *all* sickness is the result of long-term stress, emotional or physical abuse, negative thinking, and the like. I am simply saying when you are at the end of your rope and you have followed everything the doctors told you to do yet you see no change in your condition, there is an 80 percent to 90 percent chance the sickness is a result of an emotional root that needs to be dealt with so your body can heal.[2]

What Do the Professionals Say?

The CDC along with several other doctors have come out and said that 80 percent to 90 percent of all sickness is related to (in some form or another) to long-term excessive stress, emotional or physical abuse, years of negative thinking, or unforgiveness.[3] I would like to quote a few doctors' findings on this subject.

> I have long believed that emotional factors are one of the most important contributing factors for all diseases... There is overwhelming evidence that your mind does matter when it comes to preventing, or triggering, disease. The idea that your emotions impact your health and the development of disease is not new. Even the conservative Centers for Disease Control and Prevention (CDC) has stated that 85 percent of all diseases appear to have an emotional element, but the actual percentage is likely to be even higher.[4]

Dr. Mercola is a credible doctor who has been featured on the *Today Show*, ABC *World News Tonight*, CNN, *Time Magazine*, *The Dr. Oz Show*, and many other programs. He has also been on the *New York Times* bestseller list for two of his books, *The No-Grain Diet* and *The Great Bird Flu Hoax*.[5] His comments are a new revelation for some, but the concept that what we think affects our health was first revealed in the Book of Proverbs: "As he thinks in his heart, so is he" (23:7).

Another doctor I wish to quote is Dr. Lipton. He is a stem cell biologist who has been on hundreds of TV and radio programs. He was also a former medical professor at Stanford University. He wrote a book called *The Biology of Belief.* His findings have been groundbreaking in terms of how the mind affects the body in relationship to our health.[6] Below are two excerpts from Dr. Lipton's findings:

> *The Biology of Belief* is a groundbreaking work in the field of New Biology. Author Dr. Bruce Lipton is a former medical school professor and research scientist. His experiments, and that of other leading-edge scientists, have examined in great detail the processes by which cells receive information. The implications of this research radically change our understanding of life. It shows that genes and DNA do not control our biology; that instead DNA is controlled by signals from outside the cell, including the energetic messages emanating from our positive and negative thoughts. Dr. Lipton's profoundly hopeful synthesis of the latest and best research in cell biology and quantum physics is being hailed as a major breakthrough showing that our bodies can be changed as we retrain our thinking.[7]
>
> He [Dr. Lipton] says the new science of epigenetics has shown that our genes are in fact controlled and manipulated by how our minds perceive and interpret our environment. It was formerly believed by science that it is our genes themselves which dictate our traits—that our genes form who and how we are. The new findings are great news because it means that we can change many things about the way we are, including our health, by changing how we interpret events and situations which happen to us. For example Dr Lipton shows that if we interpret things in a positive way, we start living healthier and better quality lives, regardless of the genetic makeup we started with. A new attitude, positive or negative, sends new messages to the cells in our body and can actually reprogram their health and behavior. It can even change cellular structure, turning diseased cells into healthy cells.[8]

This incredible scientific research can be life changing for us! The Bible says, "My people are destroyed for lack of knowledge" (Hosea 4:6). This knowledge can potentially change your life! Science is beginning to prove that our thoughts and how we interpret our environment affects our health. The messages and thoughts that are rolling around in our head play like a tape recorder in our mind and can affect our cells and thus affect our health.

Is it important to eat right and exercise; but if we do all that and yet have negative thinking patterns, we could still be hurting our bodies. We can begin to take our life back. This is good news. Every time I read the above research, I am encouraged. There is a freedom in learning about this research—freedom because we *can choose* the thoughts that we dwell on.

Just yesterday I began to get very frustrated and even slightly grumpy because of my long to do list. I was at the kitchen sink washing dishes thinking to myself, "I have all these things to do; I won't be able to stop working until 8:00 tonight." I was dreading my day. Then it hit me, "I am healthy now. I have the energy to accomplish these chores." I remembered that there was a time when I would have given my right arm to do the mundane chores I was now complaining about. When I began to think along these lines and get thankful, I literally felt the aggravation and frustration leave my body.

You see, if we allow ourselves to live in that aggravated, frustrated state frequently, it can affect our emotional and physical health. We have knowledge that teaches us that the way we think can either harm us physically and emotionally or strengthen us physically or emotionally. The above research gives us much hope. How we perceive ourselves and our environment greatly affects bodies.

Do this two-minute exercise with me: Think of a time when you were very angry or a time when someone you were close with broke your heart. Think of a time when perhaps someone betrayed you and you were left feeling hurt and angry. Or, think of a time when you were greatly afraid and your heart started pounding and your safety felt threatened. Or, think of the worst day of your life and how you felt. As you dwell on this memory, you may notice that your body cringes a bit or you feel tense. Your body will respond to what's going on in your brain, to what you're feeling. Now think of a time when you were close to someone you love, that person who is the apple of your eye, that person who brightens up your life and makes you smile. Or, recount the best day of your life and how happy you were. Or, think of a beautiful landscape you've seen or a pretty sunrise or sunset. When you think on the positive experiences, your body relaxes and you feel lighter and more carefree, unlike when you thought on the negative experience and your body tightened and was tense.

The signals that your mind is sending your body over time can impact your cells which in turn impact your health—*for the good or the bad*. God is the Creator of our bodies. In Proverbs it says, "A merry heart does good, like medicine" (17:22). Even in the depths of sickness we can still find something to rejoice over, something for which to be thankful. We can still find some joy.

The Hypothalamus Gland

You might be wondering how the thoughts in your mind literally affect your body chemistry. There is a gland in our bodies called the hypothalamus gland. This gland connects your mind and your nervous system to the rest of the body. Your body actually listens to what's going on in your mind through the hypothalamus gland. The brain is constantly sending signals to your body through the nervous system.

> The hypothalamus gland is the link between the endocrine and nervous systems... It is responsible for maintaining your body's internal balance, which is known as homeostasis. To do this the hypothalamus helps stimulate or inhibit many of your body's key processes, including: Heart rate and blood pressure, Body temperature, Fluid and electrolyte balance, including thirst, Appetite and body weight, Glandular secretions of the stomach and intestines, Production of substances that influence the pituitary gland to release hormones, Sleep cycles. The hypothalamus is involved in many functions of the autonomic nervous system, as it receives information from nearly all parts of the nervous system. As such, it is considered the link between the nervous system and the endocrine system.[9]

Our thoughts, especially the negative ones, can adversely affect our nervous system, which then affects our physical bodies. We can see how the devil can put sickness on us. He influences our thoughts, our thoughts influence our nervous system, and our nervous system influences our bodies. Our thoughts can be a positive influence over our bodies or a negative influence over our bodies.

I want to note here that I'm not trying to explain away all sicknesses but what I am pointing out is that when you have followed all that the medical profession is telling you to do yet you still see little to no progress, perhaps it's time to take notice of what you're thinking about!

Sick Mentality

I want to bring your attention to what a sick mentality is. This is when you are so accustomed to being sick that even if God did heal your body or the doctor prescribed a healing remedy, your mind would continue to tell your body that you are sick. This is having a sick mentality.

A personal example of this is when, after I was sick for a year with a very slow recovery, my husband, children, and I decided to go on a family vacation. It was a simple vacation. We drove to another part of the country to visit relatives. All I had to do was sit or lie in a car. When we finally arrived at the relations' house,

I was occupied with visiting family members whom I had not seen in a very long time. I noticed that after about four days that I did not "feel" sick. I thought this was strange. Not much had changed physically in four days, but it was as though I forgot I was sick.

When I got back to my house, I resumed feeling just as sick as I did before the vacation. I realized that I had developed a sick mentality. My mind was used to being sick. I had to slowly change my mind and remind myself of how far I had come. I had to remind myself that I was getting better day by day. I had to fill my mind with Word of God, the Bible. I needed to start expecting to feel healthy instead of expecting to feel sick.

As I close this chapter, I want to discuss nutrition. As I was growing up, my nickname was "junk food junkie"—literally, those exact words. I would wake up and eat chocolate cake. I ate a lot of carbs and candy and *very few* fruits, vegetables, and proteins. The way I eat now is completely opposite. I now eat few carbs, nearly no sweets, and a lot of proteins, vegetables, and fruits. I have prayed for a long life, and I know I have to take care of my body. Eating right and excising is a regular part of my life. I also juice many fruits and vegetables because I know I cannot eat enough whole food in one day to provide what body needs from fruits and vegetables.

When I was eating so poorly, I was setting myself up for disaster. If you add years of poor nutrition to unresolved emotional issues, you get a substandard quality of life. For years I prayed to God, "Help me! Please help me! Why won't You help me?" God was looking down on the whole person—body, soul, and spirit—and let's just say He had His work cut out for Him. Year by year, revelation by revelation, God removed my ignorance and replaced it with His wisdom. He is the one with knowledge of how He wired the body, soul, and spirit to function in harmony. My goal is to give you, the reader, the revelation and knowledge that I had to learn the very long way.

PRAYER

God, I ask for Your wisdom, strength, and comfort as I begin this process of healing my damaged emotions. Holy Spirit, I look to You for guidance in this process. Help me to be willing and patient to look at and examine any destructive emotional roots that need to be removed. I thank You that Your desire is for me to be whole and healthy. I put my hand in Yours now and begin this process. In Jesus name I pray. Amen.

Chapter 2.
THE PRINCIPAL OF AGREEMENT
What Are You Agreeing With?

THE PRINCIPAL OF agreement can change the direction of your life, *for the better or for the worse*. We can either agree with God and what He says about us, or we can agree with Satan's lies and what he says about us. Many times we are not even aware of what we are coming into agreement with, yet the power of agreement has the potential to change our lives.

What are you putting your expectations in? What are you believing for? What truths are you agreeing with about yourself? Do you buy into such lies as: you're not as good as someone else or you're not likable, loveable, or acceptable? Perhaps you agree with negative thoughts of guilt, fear, anger, chronic sickness, etc. What you come into agreement with will eventually come to pass in your life.

The word *agreement* means to conform, to be of the same mind or the same opinion. When we agree with God, the miraculous can happen in our life. But the opposite is also true; when we agree with the devil, his will can be accomplished in our life. God has a plan for your life and Satan has a plan for your life. Don't be deceived, the devil wants to thwart God's destiny for your life. This is a simple but immensely powerful truth. The power of your agreement will govern your life and perhaps the lives of your children. Children tend to repeat the same choices and thought patterns that they learned from their parents, so understanding this principal of agreement is crucial for you and your children.

A personal example of this is when I was preparing to fly to Georgia. I was speaking to a group of women there. I knew it was a divine appointment for me to go. The morning of my flight to Georgia I was walking from my house to the car when out of nowhere I got this terrible thought that if I went to Georgia I would not be returning back home again. The thought hit me right in the stomach, and I gasped at first.

It took me a couple of minutes to realize this was a lie from the enemy. He was trying to get me to come into agreement with his lie of fear. He was trying to get me to fulfill his will for my life, which would have been for me not to go. When I realized this was the enemy, I said to myself, "*No way!*" It was clear to me if the devil was trying that hard to get me *not to go*, then it was imperative that I go. I went to Georgia and the trip went great. Looking back, I'm thankful I did not come into agreement with the devil and cancel my trip to Georgia.

This is an example of how we have to choose who and what we will come into agreement with. What we come into agreement with is what will be fulfilled or produced in our life. I would be amiss if I did not share with you that there have been times when I was not so successful. I have had numerous times in my life when I was attempting to step out and do something and I would get these horrible thoughts that if I proceeded something awful would happen. One such example was my experience with finding a lump.

The thought, the fear, the trips to the doctor

One Christmas morning I noticed a lump under my arm next to my right breast. The thoughts that were bombarding my mind were, "What if this is breast cancer? What if I have to have surgery? What if, what if, what if?" The worst case scenarios were running through my mind. My thoughts were spiraling down fast. It was Christmas morning and all doctor offices were closed.

The timing of the enemy couldn't have been any more tormenting than to throw this at me on Christmas morning. The rest of my Christmas day was filled with incredible worry and anxiety over what would happen next. Needless to say, this put a damper on my time with my family and the rest of the holiday.

As soon as I could, I went to my doctor and they ordered a series of tests. After much testing and a biopsy they found nothing. I would spend the next two years getting biopsies and in constant fear of these lumps. For the next two years my mind was bombarded with thoughts of fear and anxiety over this issue. The devil was trying to get me to come *into agreement* with him that I was going to get cancer.

Finally, after a couple of years, it dawned on me that by listening to the fearful lies of the enemy I could be making myself sick. I finally told my regular doctor that I would be faithful to get a mammogram and ultrasound each year but I was finished running to an oncologist every six months for biopsies. Even with a clean mammogram and ultrasound, the professional recommendation was that I continue to go see an oncologist. This was not necessary and it was creating a lot of anxiety. After I made this decision to stop running to the oncologist, the fear of these lumps dissolved.

You see, the devil was trying to convince me that I was going to get this illness. I had to cast down those fearful arguments. Job says, "The thing I greatly feared has come upon me" (3:25). So instead of listening to the fear that was coming from the enemy, I searched the Word of God for a scripture that would counter the enemy's lies.

Psalm 91:10 says, "No evil shall befall you, Nor shall any plague come near your dwelling." I began to quote this scripture over and over *and over* until I finally believed it. What I was doing was coming into agreement with God's Word instead of the lies of the enemy. In this area I found freedom from torment from the devil. I eventually rejected the devil's plan and began to come into agreement with God's plan.

Lust and Divorce

Let's look at agreement from the perspective of lust or divorce. It's sad to say, but I have come into contact with so many people who have been affected by either divorce or adultery. Why is divorce and adultery rampant in our society? Because the devil knows that the quickest way to destroy lives and put people in bondage is to bring betrayal and abandonment into the family unit. Divorce and adultery can scar people for their entire lives. Unless they seek out emotional healing, they will bring their past hurts into their current relationships and also pass them down to their children. The pain and brokenness that is left from divorce or adultery can lead people down a path of loneliness, depression, anxiety, drug and alcohol abuse, financial loss, and a whole host of destructive patterns. Adultery and divorce are two areas that the devil may try and tempt you or someone you love to come into agreement with him.

Remember, the devil's goal is to break up the family unit and harm individuals. The Bible describes the devil as a roaring lion that is out for our destruction: "Be sober, be vigilant; because your adversary the devil walks about like a roaring lion, seeking whom he may devour" (1 Pet. 5:8).

My grandparents got a divorce because of infidelity. This was not an acceptable practice in the 1950s Italian culture. My parents also divorced because of infidelity. Sometime after I became a Christian, the devil attempted to convince me that I would fall to similar patterns, but by God's grace I refused the devil's invitations to come into agreement with this sin.

The Bible says to cast "down arguments and every high thing that exalts itself against the knowledge of God, bringing every thought into captivity to the obedience of Christ" (2 Cor. 10:5). Divorce and adultery can be broken in your family line by *coming out of agreement* with this temptation. We need to put on the full armor of God to stand against the lies of the enemy (Eph. 6:11).

Did you know the greatest weapon the devil uses against us is a lie? This is very important because the devil knows how to bring havoc in your life by getting you to come into agreement with his lies. When or if this temptation comes your way, close the door to protect your family. Don't allow Satan to use the power of agreement in the area of lust and divorce to destroy your family.

Familiar Thoughts

Some negative thoughts are very familiar to us because they have been in our family line for generations, such as the example I just gave about divorce running in my family. (I will go into more detail about generational issues in chapter 3.)

The Principal of Agreement

In relationship to sickness, the power of agreement can greatly affect our health. The enemy of our soul knows this principle and looks for someone who has had a parent or other family member with an illness. The enemy attempts to torment the family member that they, too, will get the same sickness. This is best understood by the two true stories below.

There was a woman whose mother died of breast cancer. The daughter was so afraid of getting breast cancer like her mother that she had both breasts removed to ensure that she would not get the disease. She had *never been diagnosed with any type of cancer* yet she underwent this procedure. She feared breast cancer so much that she had parts of her body surgically removed in an attempt to protect herself.

Perhaps illness was a generational curse in her family line that needed to be broken. Perhaps her mother's cancer was due to harmful chemicals she was exposed to or some other external factor to which the daughter was never exposed. We don't know the reasons why her mother got cancer, but because of fear the daughter underwent a surgery that was perhaps unnecessary.

Why not live life in an expectation of health and not disease? Why not come into agreement with what God says about her health? If only she considered that she may not get breast cancer. If only she began to declare healing scriptures over body. Only God knows the future, but why give into the possibility of cancer when there is no evidence of cancer?

The next example is similar to the one above, but this time it has to do with a mental illness. Once again the enemy was threatening someone with the fear of getting their parent's illness. A women's father had a mental breakdown. The father began hearing voices and became very paranoid. This greatly affected his family, his job, and his entire life. Unfortunately, this man's marriage ended in divorce.

The daughter began to fear that she would have the same kind of mental breakdown. She began to come into agreement with the devil on this issue. As of this writing, that woman has not had the same experience as her father. The reason for this is in part because she has a godly mother who is praying for her and declaring God's truths to her.

But we can see where the devil would take advantage of the women in this situation. The enemy began to speak to her out of a vulnerable area in her life. He was attempting to sit on her shoulder and speak the lie that the same illness that was on her father was going to come on her. If she continued to believe these lies, the enemy would have gained an open door into her life. The enemy was trying to convince this woman to come into an agreement with a bondage that she does not have.

These two examples show how the devil takes a sensitive area in our lives and attempts to get us to come into agreement with his plans. Unfortunately, some people live their lives tormented because of the devil's lies. He sits on their shoulder whispering that they will become just like what they have feared. We need to resist the enemy if he tries to tell us that we will suffer from the same illness as our parents or other family members. "Therefore submit to God. Resist the devil and he will flee from you" (James 4:6).

We even need to be careful of the commercials we see on TV. There are countless adds that say something to the effect that one in five people will be diagnosed with x disease, virus, or heart condition. We listen to this and then our brain starts turning, "Do I have those symptoms? Will I get that same disease? The ad just said one in five people. Maybe I'm the one in five." And we begin to mull this over in our minds and think about it and half expect that we will end up like the person we saw on that TV commercial—who is most likely is a paid actor!

I hope this brings good news to you: you don't have to come into agreement with the thoughts of fear that you are going to get a dreaded disease. For those who have had sickness, anxiety, rage, divorce, lust or any other negative behaviors in their family line, this can all be broken by breaking agreement with the devil. This *is* good news!

We break those cycles by repenting to God for our thought and behaviors of coming into agreement with the negative lies from the devil. We then renounce its hellish place in our lives. We don't stop with repentance and renouncing; we then search the Scriptures to replace the lies with the truth. We meditate on truth and begin to come into agreement with God and His plan for our lives.

One way I did this was to find a scripture that applied to my situation and then say the scripture aloud every day until I believed the scripture and no longer believed the devil's threats. This takes patience, practice, and determination. God says, "So shall My word be that goes forth from My mouth; It shall not return to Me void, But it shall accomplish what I please, And it shall prosper in the thing for which I sent it" (Isa. 55:11). When you grab hold of God's Word and declare it instead of listening to the threats of the enemy, you will see change in your life.

JESUS' EXAMPLE

If we look at Jesus as our example, we will see that the devil came to tempt Jesus to get Him to come into agreement with his plans. The Gospel of Luke chapter 4 records the account.

> Then the devil, taking Him up on a high mountain, showed Him all the kingdoms of the world in a moment of time. And the devil said to Him, "All this authority I will give You, and their glory; for this has been delivered to me, and I give it to whomever I wish. Therefore, if You will worship before me, all will be Yours."
> —LUKE 4:5–7

This is the point at which Satan was trying to convince Jesus to come into agreement with his plans.

> And Jesus answered and said to him, "Get behind Me, Satan! For it is written, 'You shall worship the LORD your God, and Him only you shall serve.'"
>
> LUKE 4:8

Jesus responds so perfectly, when He says to Satan, "Get behind Me." Jesus is basically telling Satan to get lost! Jesus already knew the exact Word of God that countered Satan's lie. Jesus used the Word as a weapon against the devil. The devil was tempting Jesus to come into agreement with his will. Jesus quickly reminds the devil of God's truth, and with scripture Jesus was able to withstand the devil's will.

Wouldn't it seem odd to us if Jesus would have contemplated, even for a moment, the devil's temptation? But isn't that what we do? The devil comes to us with a lie and we say to ourselves, "Hmmm, maybe I should cheat on my spouse?" Or, "I wonder if I will get that illness?" "What if that does happen to my kids?" "What if I do lose my house?" "What if I never get free?" And so forth. Do you see where we get caught up in coming into agreement with the devil's lies? We need to learn from Jesus' example. When that first negative thought comes into our mind, we need to starve that negative thought by refusing to give it time and attention.

We are all in progress, so don't come down on yourself if you are struggling to take your negative thoughts captive. It will get easier. After learning about the principle of agreement, it is my prayer that you will monitor which thoughts you are coming into agreement with. Ask yourself if your thoughts are lining up with God's Word or the devil's lies.

PRAYER

Lord, I pray the same prayer the psalmist prayed: "Search me, O God, and know my heart; test me and know my anxious thoughts. See if there is any offensive way in me, and lead me in the way everlasting" (Psalm 139:23-24, NIV). You have written Your desires for me on my heart. Help me not to be tempted with fears that ensnare my thoughts, my heart, and my actions. These agreements bring on grief and sinfulness. God, I repent for my wrongful agreements with Satan. I thank You that I am released from these agreements. I thank You for promising to be with me, to be my strength in times of trouble and in times of temptation. Bring me into agreement with Your perfect will and plan for my life. In Jesus name I pray. Amen.

Chapter 3

ORIGINS OF NEGATIVE THOUGHTS

Our negative, toxic thoughts have their origin from mainly three sources. These origin points of our thinking can be the genesis of *all negative, toxic emotions*. We first have a thought, *then* an emotion; so if our emotions are toxic, that's because our *thoughts* our toxic. To help in understanding these key points, I have below a list that shows the three sources of our negative thinking.

It's important to understand, before we go any further in our discussion of specific toxic emotions, that we recognize the source of our toxic thoughts. As you go through the next section of this book, which contains specific toxic emotions, it will be necessary to identify where your toxic thoughts originated. You will find that the three sources of negative thinking can overlap. Take a look at the list below because I will be making references to this list throughout the book.

THREE SOURCES OF NEGATIVE, TOXIC THOUGHTS

1. Traumatic or abusive experiences that we've lived through that have changed the way we think
2. Thinking patterns that we have learned and/or inherited from previous generations
3. Demonically-inspired thoughts

TRAUMATIC OR ABUSIVE EXPERIENCES

We will first discuss how traumatic and abusive experiences can open the door to negative thoughts. Perhaps a trauma, a tragedy, a relationship breakup, or a death began the cycle of toxic thinking in your life. Negative events in our life can produce negative thinking, which can ultimately lead to a poor quality of life.

Some of us have hurts, traumas, and unresolved tragedies buried deep within our soul; and these unresolved hurts can come out in many different forms. Some may experience physical symptoms, such as migraine headaches, irritable bowel syndrome, skin issues, chronic fatigue syndrome, heart issues, etc. I know of women who were not able to become pregnant until they dealt with hurts from their past. Others may experience emotional symptoms as a result of hidden hurts, such as panic attacks, addictions, depression, anger, feelings of rejection, a guilt complex, etc.

There are many self-help techniques out there. I have tried a lot of them, but I have learned that you *can't treat* the surface symptoms without treating the hidden wounds in your soul. When the wounds in our life heal, then our surface maladies lose their grip in our lives. In dealing with my own toxic thinking, I found that once I confronted hurts and traumas things like guilt, fear, and rejection, the physical afflictions faded from my life.

To best illustrate that trauma and tragedy can change the course (for the worse) of someone's life, I am going to share *one* of the *many* roots behind the panic attacks that I experienced.

Negative thinking from my traumatic experience

I will be sharing some of my story throughout this book. For the purpose of illustrating how traumas can shape our thoughts and open the door to toxic emotions, I will discuss an event that led up to severe anxiety and panic attacks.

My parents divorced when I was about nine years old. Two years after the divorce, my mom married who I would call a monster of a man. This stepdad did not physically touch my brother and me, but rather brought psychological torment and terror into our home for two years. He would physically beat my mother, he would lock all the doors, and he would threaten us with a gun.

Even as I write this now, I know it was the grace of God that I endured this time period. During this time, my father, who was a good father, moved halfway across the country to take a job. So as a child, I thought the only source of safety I had *just left*. I remember I hated going home. I would try and be anywhere but home because of the terror and fear that awaited me. At times the fear I faced was almost unbearable. I remember having to call the police on a few occasions because the terror was so severe. I remember running and hiding under tables because my stepdad would be in one of his moods.

The irony was that when other people were around, this stepdad was a saint; but when no one was around and it was just my mother, brother, and me, he became the devil. So early on I learned this pattern: when other people were around I was safe, but when I was alone the fear would flare up. *This was the beginning of my thought patterns of fear that would follow me into adulthood.*

As a young adult, when I started having panic attacks, it was the same pattern of fear. I would have panic attacks when I was alone, but when other people were around I felt safe. There was no threat of fear when others were around; but when other people were *not* around, the panic attacks would begin. This is precisely the pattern I experienced as a child and this pattern followed me into adulthood. The coping skill I was forced to learn for my survival when I was eleven was to keep others around me and I would be safe.

When I became an adult, I did not need this coping skill, yet unfortunately this became the pattern of fear I lived even then. I did not deal with this hidden trauma until I was well into my thirties. I did not know this trauma should be dealt with; all I knew is that I was experiencing severe panic attacks.

I remember being in college and having mild anxiety. I began to see the school psychologist. I remember telling her of this experience and saying it very matter-of-fact. She tried to convince me that I needed more intense therapy, but at the time I just thought that was something I lived through and it was over now. I had no idea that about ten years later I would confront those terrorizing years and heal from them. I will discuss more on how to heal in the related chapters throughout this book.

I would ask you the question, what unhealthy patterns did you learn during a time of trauma that you're still living out today? What negative events happened to you that changed the course of your life? How have traumatic events in your life shaped your thinking today? Can your thoughts easily go into such things as anger and bitterness (chapter 10); a broken heart (chapter 5); guilt and accusation (chapter 7); self-reproach (chapter 6); worry, anxiety, or fear (chapter 8); depression (chapter 9); unforgiveness (chapter 11); or even a physical problem for which the doctors have no remedy.

If you experienced a trauma, tragedy, or broken relationships and you're experiencing one or more of the above issues, then it's no accident this book is in your hand.

PATTERNS LEARNED FROM PREVIOUS GENERATIONS

The second source of our thoughts can be learned from previous generations. Our thinking is passed down generationally. Ways of thinking and behaviors tend to run in family lines. There are families that have anger issues, fear issues, sickness issues, and/or financial issues. Remember, our *thinking* produces our *behavior*. Some might justify their own thoughts and behavior by saying, "Well, I get my temper from my dad's side." Or, "My grandmother was always sick." Or, "My aunt was a worrier." Or, "My grandfather was an alcoholic", etc. You get the idea.

Children learn thought patterns and behaviors from their family. Don't get mad at your relatives if you see similar patterns, because chances are they inherited their thought patterns too. Before you get discouraged, understand that there are also generational blessings that are passed down in our family lines. There are families that are known for their hospitality, integrity, and/or kindness. There are families that are artistic, musical, intellectual, good with finances, good cooks, good carpenters, and the list goes on. If you look back in your family line, there is a good chance you will see some similarities in their behaviors.

The goal in our lives is to remove the curses (later I will go into greater detail on how to do this) and expound on the blessings. In addition, God may want to establish a new generational blessing in your family line.

Edwards and Jukes

One of the best examples of generational blessings and generational curses is found in a comparison study between the family lines of Jonathan Edwards and Max Jukes. Both lived in the 1700s, but the two men were very different when it came to their commitment to God. A sociologist by the name of Richard L. Dugdale, who was a member of the prison association of New York, visited jails in upstate New York. He found that there were some inmates that were blood related, and he documented his findings. He would later put his research in a book entitled, *The Jukes: A Study in Crime, Pauperism, Disease and Heredity*.[1] There have since been critics of Dugdale's findings.[2]

Even so, all you have to do is look at headlines from our current newspapers to see the negative behaviors that run in families. Just the other day, splashed across the headlines, was an article that depicted three generations of criminals—a grandfather, a father, and a son.

Please note, just because one family member commits a criminal act does not automatically mean other family member will follow. The point in generational curses is that one family member sins and, unless that person repents and turns from his ways, there is a potential for a generational curse to begin in his descendants. You may say, "Why? That is unfair." The simple answer is that the family member who has committed the sin has now opened the door to the devil to work in their life and possibly the life of their children.

We will look at a scripture on this subject in just a moment, but first I would like for you to observe the contrast of the two men below. The contrast is of the Jukes family heritage and the Edwards family heritage. Max Jukes was an ungodly man and Jonathan Edwards was a godly man. The following comparison shows the difference between the choices that are made how those choices can affect generations after them.

> Max Jukes, the atheist, lived a godless life. He married an ungodly girl, and from the union there were 310 who died as paupers, 150 were criminals, 7 were murderers, 100 were drunkards, and more than half of the women were prostitutes. His 540 descendants cost the State one and a quarter million dollars. Jonathan Edwards...lived at the same time

as Max Jukes, but he married a godly girl. An investigation was made of 1,394 known descendants of Jonathan Edwards of which 13 became college presidents, 65 college professors, 3 United States senators, 30 judges, 100 lawyers, 60 physicians, 75 army and navy officers, 100 preachers and missionaries, 60 authors of prominence, one a vice-president of the United States, 80 became public officials in other capacities, 295 college graduates, among whom were governors of states and ministers to foreign countries. His descendants did not cost the state a single penny. "The memory of the just is blessed" (Prov. 10:7).[3]

This comparison shows the difference between a commitment to Christ and godly living and rejecting God and living ungodly. In the life of Jonathan Edwards we clearly see the generational blessings that are passed down in his family line. By contrast we see the generational curses that are passed down in Max Jukes family line. The Ten Commandments shed some light on generational blessings and curses as well. Tucked away in the Ten Commandments is a nugget of truth. The Bible says:

> For I, the LORD your God, am a jealous God, visiting the iniquity of the fathers upon the children to the third and fourth generations of those who hate Me, but showing mercy to thousands, to those who love Me and keep My commandments.
> —EXODUS 20:5–6

God makes the contrast between those "who hate Me" and "those who love Me." For those who love God, God will show mercy for a thousand generations; but for those who hate God, iniquity will be visited on their children into the third and fourth generations. The question arises; how do we break these negative generational curses? God shows us an example of how to break these negative patterns from our life. We are not left stuck in bondage. The first step we need to take is to be committed to Christ and to "love' Him, as it says in Exodus. In Nehemiah 9:2 we are taught how to break the power of a generational curse in our family line.

> Then those of Israelite lineage separated themselves from all foreigners; and they stood and confessed their sins and the iniquities of their fathers.

When we recognize a pattern of negativity that has been passed down from generation to generation, we can follow the example from this passage. The children of Israel stood and confessed the iniquities of their fathers. They didn't just confess their sin, but they also confessed *the sins of their fathers*.

Someone in your family line has got to repent to God and ask Him to forgive your bloodline of past sins. The Holy Spirit maybe prompting you right now that perhaps you are that person who will stand in the gap between your ancestors and your posterity. There is a prayer at the end of this chapter to do just that.

Proverbs tells us that "a curse without cause shall not alight" (26:2). This means when there is no more cause or reason for the curse, the curse will break. When we ask God to forgive the sins of our ancestors, and then we refuse to participate in that sin *with the help of the Holy Spirit*, that curse will break.

The first time I was planning to say a prayer to break generational curses in my life, I began to see pictures of horrible things that would happen to me if I said that prayer. The enemy was trying to intimidate me with horrid thoughts so I *would not say* the prayer. I had to fight through all the fearful thoughts that were coming to my mind and say the prayer anyway. I ended up saying the prayer twice.

About a week after I said that prayer, healing began in my body. God began to show me the way out of the physical affliction of adrenal fatigue that I was suffering with. That prayer was the beginning of a healing.

I have reprinted that powerful prayer to break generational curses at the end of this chapter. As you go through the chapters on the different toxic emotions and you observe that what you struggle with is the same thing that your family member(s) struggled with, you may want to come back to this chapter and say the prayer to break the generational curse in that particular area. You can absolutely say the prayer when you finish this chapter; but know that you may need to revisit the prayer as you go through this book, or perhaps even after that.

DEMONICALLY-INSPIRED THOUGHTS

The third source of our negative thoughts may be demonically inspired. This may sound surprising; but, yes, it's true: we can get our thoughts from the demonic realm. I like to use the example of the cartoon character that has a demon sitting on his shoulder whispering thoughts into his ear. Sometimes we will get a thought and think, "What a crazy thought. Where did that come from?" When this happens, there is a good chance that it was demonically inspired. We are taught from the Scriptures to stand against the devil's assault against us:

> Put on the whole armor of God, that you may be able to stand against the wiles of the devil. For we do not wrestle against flesh and blood, but against principalities, against powers, against the rulers of the darkness of this age, against spiritual hosts of wickedness in the heavenly places. Therefore take up the whole armor of God, that you may be able to withstand in the evil day, and having done all, to stand. Stand therefore,

having girded your waist with truth, having put on the breastplate of righteousness, and having shod your feet with the preparation of the gospel of peace; above all, taking the shield of faith with which you will be able to quench all the fiery darts of the wicked one. And take the helmet of salvation, and the sword of the Spirit, which is the word of God; praying always with all prayer and supplication in the Spirit, being watchful to this end with all perseverance and supplication for all the saints.
—EPHESIANS 6:11–18

This is a very popular portion of Scripture because it is a very truthful portion of Scripture. We have an enemy–the devil who is seeking our demise. In this passage we are instructed to put on the whole armor of God. This may sound easy enough, but some of us have holes in our armor. We have these holes in our armor because we have a wrong view of who God is and a wrong view of who we are in Him. The devil knows this and attacks us in our thoughts where we are most vulnerable. When we get healed in an area of toxic thinking, we begin to repair our armor. As we get healed we become less vulnerable to the devil's lies. The devil is a bully; and when he sees that the same lies no longer influence our thoughts, the assault of negative thoughts will begin to dissipate.

Let's look at an example of a hole in someone's armor. We read in the scripture above how it is the *shield of faith* that stops the fiery darts, or demonically-inspired thoughts of the wicked one. If someone had a difficult time trusting (having faith) in their earthly father, chances are they will have a more difficult time trusting and having *faith* in their heavenly Father. They will question whether or not God will actually come through for them. The devil observes this and tries to put demonically-inspired thoughts of depression, fear, or many other negative emotions into someone's mind. The devil can get away with this because they never received healing in the area of forgiving their earthly father and learning to rely on God; thus they cannot fully activate their *shield of faith* to protect themselves against the enemy.

In this scenario the person needs healing in the area of being able to trust God. Once the person receives healing in this area, the *shield of faith* activates and it can potentially shut the door to accepting the devil's lies.

This book is designed to help you heal any holes in your armor. I hope you're beginning to get the point that one of the sources of our negative thinking is demonically-inspired thoughts.

The devil spoke to Jesus

We know Jesus was fully God and fully man; He didn't have the kind of "hang ups" that we tend to have, and yet still the devil came at Jesus to try and influence Him. (The same is true for us even if we had no emotional issues, the devil would still attempt to negatively inspire us with his thoughts.) The devil spoke to Jesus and tried to convince Him of a different plan for His life. Jesus, of course, did not give the devil the time of day and was able to put the devil in his place with the Word of God. (In the same way, the devil and/or the demonic realm will attempt to influence our thoughts.) Below is the account of what and how the devil spoke to Jesus. The devil attempted to derail God's plan for Jesus, but he was unsuccessful because Jesus used the Word of God.

> And *the devil said to Him*, "If You are the Son of God, command this stone to become bread." But Jesus answered him, saying, "It is written, 'Man shall not live by bread alone, but by every word of God.'" Then the devil, taking Him up on a high mountain, showed Him all the kingdoms of the world in a moment of time. And *the devil said to Him*, "All this authority I will give You, and their glory; for this has been delivered to me, and I give it to whomever I wish. Therefore, if You will worship before me, all will be Yours." And Jesus answered and said to him, "Get behind Me, Satan! For *it is written*, 'You shall worship the Lord your God, and Him only you shall serve.'" Then he brought Him to Jerusalem, set Him on the pinnacle of the temple, and *said to Him*, "If You are the Son of God, throw Yourself down from here. For *it is written*: 'He shall give His angels charge over you, To keep you,' and, 'In their hands they shall bear you up, Lest you dash your foot against a stone.'" And Jesus answered and said to him, "*It has been said*, 'You shall not tempt the Lord your God.'" Now when the devil had ended every temptation, he departed from Him until an opportune time.
> —Luke 4:3–13, emphasis added

We see that three times the devil spoke to Jesus and three times Jesus defeated the devil with the Word of God. The devil can attempt to put toxic destructive thoughts in our mind, but like Jesus, we defeat those toxic thoughts with the Word of God.

The devil will look at what weakness has been handed down to us from previous generations and observe what traumas we've gone through, and he will try and influence our thoughts based on our weak spots. Remember, the devil's job description is "to steal, and to kill, and to destroy" (John 10:10). Once you are aware of the devil's tactics, you can better arm yourself from accepting his thoughts as your own and close this door to this source of toxic thoughts.

As you begin the next section of this book on specific toxic thoughts, you will need to keep in mind the three sources of thoughts—thoughts from a trauma or abuse, thoughts that have been passed down from previous generations, and thoughts that are demonically inspired. We can have one or all three of these origins of thoughts operating in our lives. As you go through each toxic emotion, refer back to what is the origin of the thoughts behind it.

Below is the prayer to break generational curses. As I mentioned earlier, the first time I said this prayer it was difficult to get through. I pressed through and then said the prayer a second time and meant every word of it. I encourage you to do the same. This declaration is from Neil T. Anderson's book *The Bondage Breaker*.

DECLARATION

I here and now reject and disown all the sins of my ancestors. As one who has been delivered from the power of darkness and translated into the kingdom of God's dear Son, I cancel out all demonic working that may have been passed on to me from my ancestors. As one who has been crucified and raised with Jesus Christ and who sits with Him in heavenly places, I renounce all satanic assignments that are directed toward me and my ministry, and I cancel every curse that Satan and his workers have put on me. I announce to Satan and all his forces that Christ became a curse for me (Gal. 3:13) when He died for my sins on the cross. I reject any and every way in which Satan may ownership of me. I belong to the Lord Jesus Christ, who purchased me with His own blood. I reject all other blood sacrifices whereby Satan may claim ownership of me. I declare myself to be eternally and completely signed over and committed to the Lord Jesus Christ. By the authority that I have in Christ Jesus, I now command every familiar spirit and every enemy of the Lord Jesus Christ to leave my presence. I commit myself to my heavenly Father to do His will from this day forward. In Jesus' name I pray. Amen.[4]

Part 2

Cause and Repair of Damaged Emotions

Chapter 4
STRESS

*A*h, stress; what exactly is stress? And why do we have so much of it in our lives today? Simply put, stress is generated by negative thoughts that create pressure and anxiety in our minds. Over time this pressure can lead to a mental or physical breakdown. We are a stressed-out people because we live in a state of worry, fear, depression, low self-esteem, anger, and unforgiveness, just to name a few. We can learn to reduce the amount of stress that we carry by reducing the toxic emotions that I just listed.

The key to living a more peaceful life is to get to the roots behind our negative thinking and then change how we think. This is what the following chapters are going to expose, areas in our lives that have roots that keep us stuck in the same pattern of toxic thinking. We want to expose the roots or the "whys" behind the way we think. Many times exposing the root, facing it, and grieving over it will bring healing and in turn reduce the amount of stress in our lives.

THREE STAGES OF STRESS

Dr. Hans Selye (1907–1982) was a pioneering Austrian-Canadian endocrinologist known as the father of stress research. He conducted important scientific research on the study of stress and how it affects our mental and physical health. In his research he names three stages of stress. He calls these stages of stress the General Adaptation Syndrome. In this syndrome Dr. Selye describes how our bodies handle small levels of stress and how our bodies handle greater levels of stress. He describes how we adapt to stress and how it affects our physical and mental health.[1]

Dr. Selye also taught that stress is not always bad for us.[2] There can be stress that comes from the excitement and exhilaration that we experience in life. What one person views as negative stress another may view as positive stress. For example, if two people are preparing to take a plane ride for a vacation, one person may have major anxiety about the plane ride while the other person is excited about the plane ride. The person with the anxiety may lose sleep, lose their appetite, and dread the day of the flight. This is negative stress in their life. The other person who sees the airplane ride as exciting is bubbling over with joy because it's the beginning of their vacation. This is positive stress. When each of these two people sits in that airplane to leave for their vacation, one is excited (good stress) and one is anxious (bad stress). The negative or positive stress that we experience begins in our thoughts. That's why it's important to heal our thought life so that we can experience less of the harmful negative stress.

> Dr. Selye did not regard stress as a purely negative phenomenon; in fact, he frequently pointed out that stress is not only an inevitable part of life but results from intense joy or pleasure as well as fear or anxiety. "Stress is not even necessarily bad for you; it is also the spice of life, for any emotion, any activity, causes stress." Some later researchers have coined the term "eustress" or pleasant stress, to reflect the fact that such positive experiences as a job promotion, completing a degree or training program, marriage, travel, and many others are also stressful. Selye also pointed out that human perception of and response to stress is highly individualized; a job or sport that one person finds anxiety-provoking or exhausting might be quite appealing and enjoyable to someone else. Looking at one's responses to specific stressors can contribute to better understanding of one's particular physical, emotional, and mental resources and limits.[3]

This is information we can learn from. How we interpret an experience will determine if it has a negative impact on our health or a positive impact.

Below I will describe the phases Dr. Seyle observed concerning the physical responses the body goes through when we're confronted with an excessive amount of negative stress: first is the *alarm stage*; second, the *resistance stage*, and third, the *exhaustion stage*.[4]

When I first researched this material, I quickly realized I had lived in each of these stages of stress for most of my life. I have also experienced the negative impact that stress can have on our physical body. Over the last twenty years, I have learned how to reduce the amount of stress that I allow into my life. To think we will rid ourselves completely of all negative stress would be a fallacy, but learning to stop stress from impacting our physical and mental health is possible.

There is knowledge to be gained from learning about the three levels of stress; and while Dr. Selye does a marvelous job in describing the problem of stress, it is the Holy Spirit who gives us the *wisdom* to *not allow* stress to ruin our lives. We will begin with the first stage; the alarm stage.

The alarm stage

This is the fight-or-flight response that the mind and body go into when confronted with a dangerous situation. The flight or fight response is characterized by biological changes that prepare the body to either fight off the stressor or flee from the stressor.[5]

An example of this would be if someone were to break into your home. Immediately your mind would start sending your body signals to either fight the attacker or run from the attacker. During the alarm stage (the body's fight or flight response) hormones such as cortisol, adrenaline, and noradrenalin are released to provide instant energy.[6]

These hormones send signals to your brain that you're going to need more strength, energy, and attentiveness to either fight or flee the situation. Your heart begins to pump more blood to your muscles to provide you with quick movement. Your breathing is increased to get your body ready to fight or flee. The body begins to move food through the digestive track more quickly to rid the body of waste. The stomach moves food along because a full stomach slows the body's fight or flight response down. This is why when we have fearful thoughts or situations we have digestive problems such as irritable bowel syndrome. The digestion process can be affected by stress. These are some of the bodily functions that occur when the body goes into fight or flight response.[7]

During the alarm stage your body (and mind) goes into red alert mode and prepares to protect itself. God put this first stage in place for our survival. If we are confronted with danger, there is a physical response system ready to help save and protect our lives. The problem arises when we go into the alarm stage when there is no physical threat present. Problems arise when our body goes into the flight or fight response because of our past memories or abuses. Going into the alarm stage is also problematic because our bodies were not designed to live in a constant state of threat. The alarm stage was designed to be an acute physical response to help us survive.

My experience has been that there are "triggers" that put the body into an alarmed state. A physical event such as a car accident, or fight with a family member, or (if you're like me) a bee flying at you can kick off the fight or flight response. Physical triggers are tangible real threats that threaten your safety. There are also psychological triggers that can set the mind and body into a fight or flight response. This could be your thoughts or your memories that trigger the alarm stage. Just remembering a traumatic event can cause the mind and body to go into fight or flight. This is the case in post-traumatic stress disorders. The definition of post-traumatic stress is a type of anxiety disorder that can occur after you have gone through an extreme emotional trauma that involved the threat of injury or death. Post-traumatic stress disorders deals with the memory of the event that takes you right back to the event as though you were reliving it. The body and mind will go into the fight or flight response simply by the memory of the event. I will discuss post-traumatic stress more in the chapter on fear.[8]

In my experience and the experience of others, there are triggers that can begin the alarm stage. For example, meeting new people, giving a speech, having a job interview, or perhaps going to the dentist can trigger the fight or flight response, especially if you had a bad experience once before in that same situation. Our mind will try and protect us from having another bad experience by sending the body messages to not repeat the same activity or revisit the same place. Our brain remembers the negative experience we had before and sends messages throughout the body that this is not a safe environment and you need to flee the situation.

A friend of mine lost her husband to a heart attack while he was in the hospital. This was an extremely difficult time for her. She developed a fear of going to doctors. Each time she would go to the doctor, her body would go into a flight or fight response and she would have a panic attack. This was her brain's way of keeping her safe. Her understanding was that doctors weren't safe and needed to be avoided. This of course is a lie; but to her this fear was very valid due to her traumatic experience of losing her husband while he was in the care of doctors. Her mind had subconsciously believed that doctors were in some way going to harm her and she needed to stay away from them to protect herself. Though it is understandable why she would go into a panic while at the doctors, she needed to deal with the root cause of this fear, which was losing her husband and overcoming the lie that doctors were going to hurt her.

Whether the perceived threat is physical or psychological, the body's response is the same. The alarm stage is the body's "call to arms."

The resistance stage

This is where the body goes into survival mode *while* the stressor continues. I once heard this stage described as when your foot is on the accelerator pedal of the car and the car doesn't know how to slow down or stop. To be healthy our "car" has to slow down, stop, and rest. Our mind and body need rest. Jesus understood this and told His disciples to come aside and rest awhile.

> And He [Jesus] said to them, 'Come aside by yourselves to a deserted place and rest a while." For there were many coming and going, and they did not even have time to eat.
> —Mark 6:31

In this stage the body attempts to adjust to the stressor as best it can. During the resistance stage, the body attempts to return to a normal biological state by restoring the energy that was used from the stress. The body is also trying to repair any damages due to the excess stress.[9] Unfortunately, the stress level remains high, although not as high as during the alarm stage. The mind still recognizes the stressor and sees the stressor as a threat.[10] This stage occurs because we cannot resolve or make peace with the problem we are facing. We keep turning the problem over and over again in our minds, and the mind and body get little relief.

The prolonged release of stress hormones may be accompanied by such emotional responses as anger, fatigue, and irritability. If a stressful condition persists or negative thought patterns persists, your body adapts by continually trying to resist the surge of negative stress hormones.[11] We are in a continual battle when the negative circumstance or thoughts do not subside.

In the resistance stage your body *does not fully recover* and allow itself to get back to homeostasis. Homeostasis is when the body is in balance and rest.[12] Unfortunately, many people live their life in this stage. The intense fight or flight response has calmed down, but there is an underlying stressor or problem that is constantly present to eat away at us. This constant stressor can affect the person right down to the cellular level.[13] Some physical symptoms may start to surface such as; trouble sleeping, muscle tension, digestion problems such as stomach aches, constipation, headaches/migraines, irritability, and a general sense of feeling down.[14] These symptoms may manifest as the body is trying to deal with the stressor.

The exhaustion stage

The third stage is the exhaustion stage. If the stressor persists, the body may enter in the exhaustion stage. Now, you may be thinking the exhaustion stage is where you're tired all the time or dragging through your day; but the exhaustion stage can be far worse than feeling tired. This is where you are so drained and depleted that you are now open to major illnesses. The immune system is greatly impaired at this stage due to the ongoing release of stress hormones.[15] The body's ability to resist disease at this stage is lost because its adaptation energy supply is gone,[16] meaning the body has been so busy fighting stress that it has not been able to use its energy to fight off infection and disease.

It's at this stage of burnout that we see people who are continually getting colds or infections. Their body is spending all its energy on the stressor with little left to fight off viruses, infections, and the like. Heart rate and respiration are now decreased to conserve bodily resources. With continued exposure to stress, the body's resources may become seriously depleted.[17] At this stage the body is functioning on low, performing only necessary functions. Stress-related disorders such as kidney disease, heart disease, allergic conditions, digestive disorders, and depression, chronic fatigue may occur.[18] The list could go on and on.

As I have already discussed, I have been at this stage twice in my life. There was a time when I was in the exhaustion stage that I was housebound for almost a year. I remember I hardly had enough energy to yawn. Friends or family had to come in and cook meals, clean the house, and do the laundry. As one who enjoyed providing nice meals and a clean home for my family, this was extremely difficult. I have learned some hard lessons from living through the stages of stress, and it is my desire to write this book so that others may learn how to avoid or how to recover from these types of adversities.

THREE SPIRITUAL STAGES OF STRESS

There is a spiritual war that wages against us to keep us in a state of continual stress. The enemy has been around humanity for a very long time and knows how to bring stress on us from a spiritual perspective. As I was contemplating the three stages of stress, I began to compare the physical stages of stress to the spiritual stages of stress in our life. Below is a description of the spiritual stages of stress and how they can impact our mind and body.

The alarm stage from a spiritual perspective

The first stage, the alarm stage, can be likened to the bully (the devil) coming to threaten us with thoughts of fear, sadness, anger, unforgiveness, and the like. When the enemy roars and whirls his lies in our mind, then the body responds by going into the stress response of fight or flight. The spiritual dynamic of the enemy's lies can trigger the physical stress response in our physical body. I have described above the stress hormones that are released and all the physical changes that can occur in the body when presented with a threat. The enemy knows this and triggers the threat. He does this by getting us to believe his lies. He understands that our physical body and our mind will be negatively affected.

I speak from experience when I tell you that there were many times the enemy would whisper fearful thoughts in my mind; and as a result my heart would race, my blood pressure would rise, cortisol and adrenal would be released, and my stomach would be in knots *all because* I was fighting a spiritual battle.

The resistance stage from a spiritual perspective

The second stage, known as the resistance stage, can be likened to the bully (the devil) coming to live in your house, meaning the devil has presented you with a constant threat or problem. This problem seems impossible, like it will never go away. This can go on for days, weeks, months, or even years. We try and find a way to cohabitate with the problem, but the problem begins to wear us out. Our mind and body attempt to find a level of peace, but the enemy is still around in the form of the "problem" or affliction. During the resistance stage, our spirit, soul, and body are trying to recover but the problem is still present. We are living with the enemy.

The exhaustion stage from a spiritual perspective

The third stage, known as the exhaustion stage, can be likened to the person becoming completely depleted and hopeless. At this stage we are ready to give up, and some even consider suicide. It's at this point that the enemy looks bigger than God. There seem to be no solutions to our problems and life looks bleak. At the exhaustion stage there is little energy left to fight the enemy, and any spiritual vigor that we once had is now gone. At this stage we are in desperate need of an intervention by the Holy Spirit.

It's at this phase that the person, Christian or not, says to God, "If You're real, I need You to intervene; because if You don't, I will die here." We feel like we are drowning in an ocean of affliction. The good news is that when we choose to turn to God through prayer, reading the Bible, and by surrounding ourselves with godly people, we find strength.

This is the truth! I know because I have lived this. This is where we find Jesus reaching out His hand to pull us out of deep waters. God's rescuing love and restoring power will begin to change us from the inside out. I have been at this stage, and I have seen miracles—the miracle of God either rescuing me out of the affliction or little by little walking me through the affliction.

When you are in the midst of the trial and don't know what to do, begin to put one foot in front of the other and keep walking, or crawling if necessary, until you begin to see freedom. God will walk you right out of the problem and right into a better quality of life.

I have presented the problem of stress to you, and you may have even seen yourself in the three stages of stress. But now I want to provide practical and further spiritual keys that will help you better deal with stress. I have over twenty years of experience in dealing with stress and all that comes along with stress. The difference for me now is that I no longer cohabitate with stress. Stress still knocks on my door, but it no longer lives in my house. I don't take stress out to dinner with me. And stress is not allowed to fall asleep with me or attach itself to me.

It is my prayer that you will benefit from the information below on how to reduce your stress levels.

STEPS TO REDUCE STRESS

As we have learned, stress can send a cascade of stress hormones into the body and over time this can lead to illness. I am going to outline a few practical steps that can alleviate stress and spiritual steps to alleviate stress. As I said at the beginning of this book, always get the advice of your doctor to counsel you on your specific needs.

I have been under the care of both regular medical doctors and also naturopathic physicians. Both were helpful; but in my journey back to health,

I discovered a clash between medical doctors and the synthetic drugs they prescribe and naturopathic doctors and the vitamins and minerals they recommend. A naturopathic doctor once told me that if you give the body natural supplements the body knows what to do with those herbs, vitamins, and minerals; but if you give the body synthetic drugs, the body may reject the foreign chemical. I encourage you to do your own research to discover what's best for your body.

B Vitamins

B vitamins can be lost during prolonged periods of stress. I speak personally only from the plethora of doctors who advised me to take vitamin B supplements. Years of stress on the body can take its toll on many internal systems of the body, particularly the nervous system. When I began to take the B vitamins, I noticed my alertness improved and my energy levels recovered. If you're someone that has a lot of stress in your life you may want to have your B levels checked. As a side note: when I had my B vitamins checked by my regular MD, he said my B levels were normal; but when my naturopathic doctor looked at those same B levels, he said my B vitamins were on the "low end" of normal and should be much higher for optimum health. The naturopathic doctor was correct; because once I started taking the vitamin B supplements, I saw a positive change.

Hormones

Stress can take its toll on our hormones. I would encourage anyone who battles stress to see your doctor and get your hormones tested. In my experience, stress is especially hard on the adrenal glands and the thyroid. There are supplements that can help rebuild both. The adrenal glands are a particular focus because during stress the adrenals work over time and when the adrenals are not functioning properly there are adverse affects in the body.[19] I took supplements for both the adrenal glands and the thyroid, and the supplements improved the functions of both.

Balanced diet and reduced sugar intake

Eating a balanced diet is necessary to maintain good health. Good food provides health to the mind and body. There is no way around this truth. When choosing what to eat, look for foods that are closer to nature, uncooked fruits and vegetables are the best. Frozen vegetables and fruits are a good second choice to fresh fruits and vegetables.

I juice a couple of times a week to help my intake of fresh fruits and vegetables. I have found this very helpful in being able to eat enough fruits and vegetables in the course of my week. One of the worst types of foods we can eat is processed foods. Processed foods may contain harmful chemicals that the body is unfamiliar with, and these chemicals can do damage to the body. Chemicals that we consume through processed foods can be destructive to us over a long period of time resulting in illness and disease. Someone once told me that *live food equals a live body*, as opposed to overcooked, processed foods.

Science teaches us that excess sugar can do damage to our bodies. We know that large quantities of sugar can suppress our immune system.[20] Having said that, I believe it is fine for most people who are eating a healthy, well-balanced diet to a splurge with dessert on occasion; but always follow the advice of your doctor.

Something to look forward to

Another way to combat stress is to have something to look forward to. Life gets busy and we are confronted with issues and situations that require us to problem solve, so it's good to give your mind and body a break! Your body chemistry changes when your brain is focused on something positive.[21] That's why it's a benefit to have an activity that you are looking forward to. It could be a vacation you are planning, going out with friends, taking a hike, going shopping, playing a sport, getting a manicure—whatever it is that brings you joy (within reason, of course), allow yourself some fun and R & R.

Exercise

Yes, this is also something we have heard for years; and it's true, exercise contributes to a healthy body. I have heard it said that if exercise could be bottled into a pill, it would be the most widely prescribed pill. The key is to find an activity that you enjoy. The exercise that you choose doesn't have to be excessive to the point where you can't talk through the activity but some type of activity that gets the body moving. Get creative with your activities; chase your kids around the house, go to a park, play Frisbee, do garden work, walk your dog—you get the idea.

There is also the option of joining a gym for exercise. Before you say you would never join a gym, you might want to give it a try. I was in my forties when my daughters finally talked me into joining a gym. I remember the day we pulled into the gym parking lot. I wanted to run the other way. All I could imagine is very fit, toned young people; and here I was a middle-aged woman. It took a few visits for me to be convinced, but now I'm hooked. Much to my surprise they gym was filled with all ages, shapes and sizes. I absolutely love how I feel after the workout. Before I exercise I feel like a rubber band that is being stretched to its maximum capacity, but after exercise I feel like the tension from that stretched rubber band is gone.

The point is to get some type of physical exercise because exercising releases endorphins and reduces the stress hormones.[22]

Stretching

This is one of my favorite things that *quickly* releases tension and stress in my body. Stretch your muscles and hold the stretch for about 10 seconds. If you will take a few minutes to stretch the major muscles groups in your body you will notice you feel relaxed afterward. Your body will feel more at ease and stress free.

Proper breathing

This is also an important step that I find can immediately stop the stress response in the body. Breathe in for two long seconds and then breathe out for four long seconds. Put your hand right above your naval and you should feel your stomach move up and down as you breathe.

It is not good if you breathe out of your neck and upper chest area. Breathing rapidly out of your upper chest and neck area is what causes people to hyperventilate. When I feel myself get nervous, I automatically start this type of deep breathing. Counting is also helpful. As you *take in a breath*, count *one* one thousand, *two* one thousand. Then as you breathe out, count *one* one thousand, *two* one thousand, *three* one thousand, *four* one thousand. This sends a message to your brain to immediately calm down. This really works!

Nature

If you're in a stressful mind-set and you need to find some peace, observe nature. I've noticed that all seasons—winter, spring, summer, and fall—have beauty in them. When you look for the beauty in nature, you will find it.

I like to look at a sunset or sunrise, squirrels in the fall, or birds in the spring. I like to watch the sun beaming through the trees or the beauty of the clouds in the summer sky. God designed the world beautifully. Not long ago I was helping my husband shovel snow. The sun was setting and the sky was filled with blues, pinks, and purples; the winter sky was breathtaking. I felt so blessed to be outside at that moment.

When you observe the beauty in nature it brings tremendous peace to the mind.

Talk or write

When you've had a lot of stressors, talking to a good friend or counselor can be extremely beneficial. We find answers to our problems when we begin to talk about what is bothering us. I have noticed that when I open up and begin to talk about a situation, harmful emotions surface and are brought out. This is healthy for us, even if tears are a result of us talking. This is healing.

Another helpful tip for getting stress out of your life is to write your concerns and feelings out on paper. A counselor once told me to write about a troublesome situation—*and then throw the paper away*. This is the same principal as talking it out; because when we get those feelings out and bring them into the light, stress levels decrease and hurts are exposed so they can be healed This process is freeing to the mind.

Five-minute break

Remove yourself from the stressful situation if possible. This will help you process information and not react illogically. If you're at work and you feel stressed, take five minutes out. Take a bathroom break, drink some cold water, sit down, and do the above breathing exercises I mentioned. Be kind to yourself and give yourself a few minutes to regroup and refresh your mind.

SPIRITUAL STEP TO REDUCE STRESS

The above are practical steps that are helpful to reduce stress, but it's equally important to seek out spiritual steps to reduce stress. This next section deals with spiritual keys to close the door on harmful stress.

Pray

That's obvious, right? Pray! If you find yourself in a battle of stress and you feel your body responding to the stress, stop what you're doing, stop what you are thinking, and ask the Holy Spirit for help. There have been countless times I have had an "emergency" come up; and instead of going into the fight or flight response, and instead of allowing my mind to race to all the worst case scenarios, I will begin to call on the Holy Spirit for help. The Holy Spirit is faithful to either calm us down or bring an answer that will settle the situation.

In the corporate world, where my husband worked for many years, he would have seasons of high stress on his job. We would pray together. Our prayer was that God would either change my husband's perspective on a stressful situation or change the negative people who were creating the stress. Yes, there were times when God would change my husband's perspective about a situation; but I saw countless times when God would *remove* the negative people who were creating the stress. Prayer does work, and God hears us when we call on Him.

If you feel you are in stress, you can cry out to God and ask Him to open your eyes to see the root of the problem. You can ask the Holy Spirit to give you insights on how to walk through your problems, You can ask Him to surround you with godly people and godly teaching that will give you fresh hope and expectation of His deliverance in your life.

When you pray you are admitting that you don't have the answer and you need God to intervene. In Philippians 4:6–7 Paul tells us:

> Be anxious for nothing, but in everything by prayer and supplication, with thanksgiving, let your requests be made known to God; and the

peace of God, which surpasses all understanding, will guard your hearts and minds through Christ Jesus.

What I love about this scripture is that it admonishes us not to worry about anything, not to stress about anything, but instead to pray. Not only are we instructed to pray, but we are instructed to pray with thanksgiving. The next part encourages us that the peace of God will guard our hearts and minds through Christ Jesus. What a tremendous promise from God! When you're stressed out and don't know where to turn, pray. God has the answer.

Other Access Points

Old wounds
Our experiences will shape how we view our world and how we think. If we have had negative experiences (particularly as a child), then we will tend to view life through broken, toxic emotions. When we view life through toxic emotions, we will have more stress in our lives. The next six chapters deal with toxic emotions and their roots. Roots that I will be identifying are such emotions as a broken heart, self-rejection, guilt, anger, bitterness, fear, depression, and unforgiveness.

If you have any one of these toxic emotions, then chances are your life is stressful. When the enemy knows you're broken in one of these areas, he will come to whisper thoughts in your mind that will create stress in an area in which you broken. You are more susceptible to stressful thinking if you still have open wounds. For example, if you have an issue with guilt, the enemy will tell you all the things that you're not doing and how you should feel guilty. He will tell you that you are not measuring up and you're a failure. This train of thought can lead to stress. I address specifics on how to deal with the root of guilt in the corresponding chapter on guilt. Each chapter is designed to help you break free from wounded emotions.

But for our purposes, the best way to get started in closing the door of stress in your thinking is to practice the stop sign method that I mentioned in the introduction. In the stop sign method, when you get a negative stress thought and you feel your mind *and body* begin to spiral down, *hold up a stop sign in your mind.*

There have been countless times where a negative stressful thought will enter my mind and I will envision a stop sign and say no to that thought. I will not roll that thought over and over in my mind. This in turn reduces the amount of stress in my mind and body. Just recently I was walking to my car and I got the thought that I was all alone and what if? I held up that red stop sign in my mind and I said, "Not today, devil! I am not going to fall for that lie and get myself into fear.

Not today am I going to allow that thought to kick off the fight or flight stress response and send a surge of stress hormones in my body."

Do you see how that stops sign works? As you get healing in a particular area of negative thinking, holding up that stop sign will get easier and easier. That is why prayerfully reading the chapter that pertains to your area of brokenness is so important. The Holy Spirit wants to help you in your area of weakness, and He wants to bring new levels of freedom to your life.

The occult

The enemy can have a legal right into our lives if we have dabbled in the occult. Participating in the occult can include going to palm readers or fortune tellers, practicing witchcraft, playing the Ouija board, watching movies that were inspired by the demonic, and the like. The source of these practices and where they get their information from is of the devil. It is a bit of a double standard to go to the devil for guidance (as in the case of fortune tellers) and then ask God to help us in our afflictions. We need to choose one side or the other. Either we are going to get into agreement with God (His Word, the Bible) or we are going to get into agreement with the devil.

If you have participated in any form of the occult, repent to God and ask Him to forgive you and cleanse you from your involvement with the occult. Ask the Holy Spirit to shut any door that you may have opened to the devil.

Make a commitment to God the Father, God the Son, and God the Holy Spirit to serve Him and not the enemy. Make a decision to live for God and ask the Holy Spirit to guide you into peace and out of stress thoughts.

IN CONCLUSION

It takes time to change the habit of stress. As you go through the remainder of this book, you will uncover the cycles of negativity in your life and ways to break free from these patterns. The list below shows the progression of negative roots in your life.

- Negative roots (from hurts in our past or current crises) produce
- Negative thinking, which produces
- Toxic emotions, which produce
- Negative behaviors, which produce
- A poor quality of life.

Once the source of the negative roots is exposed and dealt with, you will be less susceptible to stress. Below is a prayer to ask God for wisdom to deal with the stress in your life.

> *Heavenly Father, I ask You to help me get to the source of my stress. As I begin this journey of healing from negative thinking, show me the stumbling blocks that have kept me bound. Give me the strength to go from the surface issue to the root of the issue. Grant me the wisdom to know which remedy I need to overcome a stressful situation. God, I also seek Your grace to heal my mind, body, and spirit. I look to You, Holy Spirit, for Your counsel as I begin this process of restoration. Thank You in advance for the good things that You have in my future. In Jesus' name I pray. Amen.*

Chapter 5
BROKEN HEART

When I was a child I remember hearing my relatives recount the story of how my great grandfather's mother died of a broken heart. My grandfather came to America as a young man seeking a better life. Unfortunately, he left behind several siblings and a very brokenhearted mother. After my great-grandfather got settled into a job and a new life, he began sending money back to Italy for his grieving mother to come to America. Unfortunately the money never made it to his mother. The money that my grandfather sent back to Italy was intercepted by a family member. His grieving mother never saw the money and never saw her son again. And so the story goes that she eventually died of a broken heart. I began to wonder if someone could actually die or have health problems because of a broken heart. I began to do research to find out if there could be a connection between a broken heart and our health?

What I have since learned is, yes, we can have health problems due to a broken heart. There is actually a medical term called, "stress cardiomyopathy," which is the medical term for broken heart syndrome. Science does confirm that stress can actually affect the functions of the heart. Let's weigh in on what the experts say, and then we will learn what the Bible says.

> People with broken heart syndrome may have sudden chest pain or think they're having a heart attack. These broken heart syndrome symptoms may be brought on by the heart's reaction to a surge of stress hormones. In broken heart syndrome, a part of your heart temporarily enlarges and doesn't pump well, while the remainder of the heart functions normally or even with more forceful contractions. Broken heart syndrome may be caused by the heart's reaction to a surge of stress hormones. The condition may also be called takotsubo cardiomyopathy, apical ballooning syndrome or stress cardiomyopathy by doctors. The symptoms of broken heart syndrome are treatable, and the condition usually reverses itself.[1]
>
> Sidney Smith, a cardiologist at the university of North Carolina and spokesman for the American Heart Association...says broken

heart syndrome, which often is misdiagnosed as a heart attack, ultimately will account for a fraction of the 7 million heart attacks that occur in the USA each year.[2]

"It is a fact that grief can lead to death. It is also true that a loss, or grief, or depression can lead to changes in the immune function," explains says Robert Ader, PhD, a distinguished university professor at the University of Rochester School of Medicine and Dentistry's department of psychiatry...Stress can suppress the immune system, and the lack of basic things like sleeping and eating could not be good for a person's general health.[3]

After researching several medical opinions on this subject, I found that a broken heart can affect our health and even temporarily affect the way our heart functions. There are many other studies that confirm that a broken heart does impact our health.

But let's take a look at another source, the Bible. The Bible teaches us what science is now discovering: what we think and the condition of our soul does affect our physical body. The Book of Proverbs says, "A merry heart does good, like medicine, But a broken spirit dries the bones" (17:22). There are tremendous keys to good health that can be found in this one verse. This verse has become one of my favorite verses in the Bible concerning health, and I will explain why.

THE MERRY HEART

The first part of this verse equates a merry heart, a happy heart, to medicine. If we have a joyful disposition, if our heart is free from major stressors and sadness, it's like taking good medicine. Having a merry or happy heart can result in the following physical changes:

- A reduction in the stress hormones cortisol and adrenalin
- A release of endorphins which helps the immune system[4]
- Laughter is a good workout for the heart:
- It reduces pain,
- It lowers blood pressure, and
- It improves breathing.[5]

God, our Creator, knew that keeping our mind in peace and joy would yield health benefits to our body. The merry heart is like *medicine*. In the original Hebrew language of the Bible, the word *medicine* means, a cure, a healing, or the healing of a wound. This verse is teaching us that a *joyful heart can result in a cure and healing*. A smile, a laugh, a joyful disposition can be healing for our mind and body. This is a powerful truth found in the Word of God.

Keep in mind that joy and laughter need to be a way of life. Perhaps living with joy seems unfamiliar to you. Let me encourage you that the way you think is a habit, and habits can be changed. It has been said that it takes about thirty days to develop a new habit. Begin to look for what you can be "merry" about. Many times I reflect back how God has been faithful to me. I will observe the beauty in nature or the blessing of my children. Look for little things that put a smile on your face and bring joy to your heart. Look for opportunities to laugh.

When I was very sick, I would go on the computer and look up babies giggling or singing because God was teaching me about getting more laughter into my life. In times of emotional or physical affliction, it's imperative that we turn our attention to joy. When life does not turn out the way we anticipate, find something to be thankful for.

Staying focused on God's good news for our life will also be medicine for our bodies. There may be people who bring misery to your life; pray about how much time you should spend in their company. Guard your heart against feeding on the negativity that has the potential to come into our home through television. When I see other people's grief and sorrow on TV, I pray for them and ask God to comfort them. We can have compassion for others and when we have the opportunity to help we should, but we cannot daily carry others' sorrows.

THE BROKEN SPIRIT

Let's look at the second part of this verse. God uniquely equated a broken spirit (a broken heart) to drying up bones. Before you say to yourself, "What do bones have to do with our overall health?" let me explain. In our bones there is flexible tissue called bone marrow. The bone marrow is responsible for the production of blood cells—red blood cells, white blood cells, and platelets.[6]

I want to focus in on the white blood cells. Another name for white blood cells is leukocytes. The main function of the leukocytes is to fight infections—bacteria, viruses, fungi, and tumors. Some of these cells are also referred to as T cells, B cells, and natural killer cells. When a person has an infection in their body, their white blood cell count can be elevated, signaling that the body is fighting an invader.[7]

The body's main defense originates in the bones. In the bones is where our body's military is located to fight invaders! To break it down very simply, our immune system starts in the bones. It is through the bones that our health is protected. This area of our bodies needs to be healthy to protect us. The Bible is teaching us that a *broken heart* dries up the *bones*, the broken heart dries up our body's ability to fight off infections. The broken heart impairs our immune system.

Broken spirit in the Hebrew means a stricken heart, a wounded heart, an afflicted spirit, or a sad spirit. According to *Merriam-Webster*, the definition of *broken* is to stop working because of being damaged. When I read that definition, I was struck with awe to think that our immune system can be damaged because someone broke our heart.

If you are someone that has struggled with a poor immune system and you have tried many medical treatments and your immune system is still not working properly, then I would ask the following questions: Has someone broken your heart? Have you ever experienced a loss that left your heart in pieces? Did you ever recover from that loss? Do you hear a song on the radio and it takes you right back to the pain of that failed relationship? Or, do you perhaps avoid going somewhere because it reminds you of that person?

You see, this is how the enemy uses the events in our lives to continue to break our hearts and bring illness to our bodies. Don't forget that the body responds to the emotions that are going on in our minds. And if those emotions are damaged, over time the body responds to those damaged emotions and we get sick. If you have had your heart broken and you have a strong immune system, thank God! Let this word be "prevention" for you because you do not want brokenness to affect your body; but if your heart was broken and you suffer from emotional or physical problems, then perhaps it's time to get that broken heart healed. God wants to heal your broken spirit and give you a merry heart!

Turmoil or Peace

The reality is that a joyful disposition or sorrowful disposition can specifically affect our immune system. God, the designer of our bodies, knew this all along. The enemy of our soul, the devil, also knows that a heart filled with brokenness can affect our health. When someone hurts us, the enemy is there to constantly remind us of what they did wrong and how unforgivable their deed was. He wants to make sure that the pain is deeply rooted in our soul. He wants to make sure that we replay this sadness over and over in our minds by triggering our memories. Our painful memories force us to relieve the hurt.

I did a study once on the demoniac that Jesus healed. (See Luke 8:26–39.) The scripture tells us that the demon possessed man lived in the tombs. If you study that word translated *tombs* in the original Greek, the root word is *memories*. You see, the demon possessed man lived in his memories. When we live in our memories, we open the door to the devil tormenting our minds, which in turn can put sickness on our body. Oh, let that be a lesson for us not to live in our memories lest we open the door to the devil! The devil knows that a *broken heart can dry up your immune system.*

Remember, Jesus said in the Gospel of John that the enemy comes "to steal, and to kill, and to destroy" (John 10:10). That is his job description. He has been around mankind long enough to know that brokenness can bring havoc into a person's mind and body. The devil knows how to put sickness on a person. It has become clear to me how the devil works overtime on people and this in turn opens the door to mental and physical sickness. Enough! It's time to understand the enemy's strategies against us and one of those strategies is to keep us brokenhearted.

God wants to heal that broken heart and bring joy back into your life. How can a broken heart be healed? Let's keep going.

PERSONAL EXPERIENCES WITH A BROKEN HEART

A difficult good-bye

As I was learning about the connection between the condition of our soul and the immune system, I was remembering the first time my heart was broken. It was the kind of emotional pain that felt like I had been punched in the stomach. The first time I ever experienced that gut-wrenching pain was when I was eleven. My parents had been divorced when I was ten, and I was getting along okay. But my first experience with real heart pain was when life's journey took my dad to another state. In the eyes of an eleven-year-old, he might as well have moved to another country. I remember the day he left very vividly. After he said good-bye and drove off, I spent the next several hours in my room crying and crying *and* crying. To me my source of strength and protection was leaving.

I do not fault my dad because he followed his own path. Unfortunately, that path was thirteen hours away, and I was left completely brokenhearted. I was able to spend my summers with my dad. But at the end of every summer there was always that dreaded day: the day when I would hug my dad good-bye, knowing that I would not see him again for long time. This was extremely painful and heartbreaking, and every year it was the same scenario. At the end of the summer, he would drive me to the airport. I would have to hold back crying in front of him. He would hug me good-bye, and I would board the plane. Once on the plane the airline stewardesses must have seen the dreaded good-bye scenario, because they would unsuccessfully try to comfort me. This went on year after year.

Even into adulthood when I had to say good-bye to my dad after a visit that dreaded pain would easily resurface. I was always an emotional wreck after having to say good-bye to my dad, even as an adult. It would not be until my late thirties that I would break free from this strong painful emotion. But it's important to note that I *did* eventually break free.

What led to the healing? you might ask. Over time I was able to realize that my dad loved me no matter what his address was. His leaving when I was eleven was in no way a rejection of who I was. Children wrongly assume that parents move or leave because the child is not valued; many times this is not true. With the realization that my father loved me (I learned later that he tried to get custody), helped to heal my heart in this area. Talking about and releasing this pain also helped bring healing. And I will tell you, when I faced this pain in my heart head on, it was like a well of tears was opened inside my soul and I felt like I could cry for days. Letting all this pain out of my heart was imperative. This is a key; facing the pain and grieving over the pain, and knowing that you can still be a complete and whole person despite your loss. The worst thing we can do is stuff that pain because it will come out in other ways. Healing was a process, but restoration in this area did come.

The next time that I faced that gut-wrenching heartbreak was when I was eighteen. I was seeing a young man that I thought I would marry. We began to date, and I very quickly fell in love with this person. At the time I felt that I could only be happy if I was with him. After a considerable length of time, we broke up.

I was in such turmoil and heartbreak that I no longer wanted to be in the same city with him. Everything reminded me of him, and the memories were intensely painful. I was so broken that I decided to move halfway across the country to escape how I felt. I thought if I could just move away, the heart pain would ease. Unfortunately, moving did not heal my heart. I had put this young man on a pedestal and created my own identity from our relationship. When the relationship fell apart, so did I.

I did not grieve over this heart pain until many, many years later because I stuffed it so carefully, I did not even know I was walking around with a broken heart. Once again, I had to confront this pain, cry over this pain, talk about this pain, and journal about this pain until the memory of the pain no longer brought a sting to my soul.

The lie about God

Another time I felt a broken heart was actually toward God. Have you ever wrongly perceived or wrongly thought that God had disappointed you? I felt brokenhearted because I "thought" *God had let me down.* I had been waiting years for a promise from God to be fulfilled. One evening I found out that the very promise that I had been so patiently waiting for had been achieved in someone else's life. I was very happy for them, but I felt utterly and completely devastated. I felt like God had passed me over and rejected me. I remember very distinctly the brokenhearted feeling that came over me. I thought to myself, "God, You have truly broken my heart." I went home devastated and went to sleep devastated.

I woke up the next morning and read the *Daily Bread* devotional as I frequently do. I read it out of habit, not desire. The short devotional spoke of Eve in the Garden of Eden. The author discussed how the devil put lies into Eve's mind to get her to distrust God. His goal was to get her to believe that God was withholding something. Then it hit me like a ton of bricks: "Aha! The enemy is using the same strategy on me that he used on Eve. He was trying to get me to believe that God was holding out on me, that God was withholding something good from me. I had been duped by the enemy just like Eve. I bought the lies the devil was whispering to me that God was cruel and uninterested in my feelings. I bought it. Not only did I buy it but I took it home and kept this lie close to me.

As soon as I finished reading that commentary, I immediately repented to God and asked Him to forgive me for believing the devil's lies. I made a commitment to God that day that I would trust His love and plan for me. After that experience I found a new trust for God. Although the enemy attempted to convince me that God had broken my heart, that experience made me trust and love Him even more.

In Closing

We all experience times when our heart feels as though it has been crushed. Grieving the loss of a relationship is extremely important. If you feel stuck in this area, I would encourage you to first answer the question: Who (or what life circumstance) broke your heart? After you answer that question, get out a piece of paper and begin to pour out your soul onto that paper, writing out all the details surrounding that time in your life. You may even want to share your broken heart with a friend or a Christian counselor.

I spent time in tears, crying over the loss and hurt I felt. And after all the writing, talking, and crying, I gave the pain over to God. I saw myself putting my pain on the cross of Jesus Christ and then I asked Him to heal my heart. I understood that I was no longer a victim to this pain. I understood that my identity was no longer defined by this pain. I also understood that I could take my experience with heartbreak and help others.

Perhaps all our questions may not be answered surrounding our heartbreak. In the Bible God is called Jehovah Rapha, our healer. *Rapha* in the original Hebrew means to heal by stitching or sewing back together again. That is His nature—He is a healer, and He will heal our hearts.

There were times when that season of hurt in my life would get brought up again, but the sting of hurt was no longer attached to that memory. This is a process, and everyone's healing process is different. Don't get discouraged while in the process.

I have also provided a companion workbook (available at www.luanndunnuck.

com) as a helpful tool in discovering the roots of your broken heart. Know that God wants to heal your broken heart. Below is a prayer to help you give your hurts over to God and begin the healing process.

Prayer

God, You see the hurts buried deep in my heart. Father, give me the courage to face and grieve over the emotional pain I have been carrying. Holy Spirit, I ask You to be with me as I allow myself to examine painful areas from my past, and I ask You to show me any roots that need to be removed from my heart. I make a decision to put my heartbreaks on your alter and not to pick them up again. Help me to lend forgiveness to others so I can move forward in freedom. I desire to be free of a heavy heart, and I want to be able to love others without bringing baggage from my past into my current relationships. I'm tired of living my life from a place of pain, and I am ready for the healing process to begin. Lord, I look to You to bring me step-by-step into liberty and to bring healing to my body, soul, and spirit. I pray, Holy Spirit, that You would supernaturally restore my physical body as my soul begins to heal (3 John 1:2). In Jesus' name I pray. Amen.

Chapter 6

SELF-REPROACH

Do you ever find yourself in thought patterns of shame and self-disapproval? Do you ever criticize your actions or words? Are you disappointed with areas of your life or feel like a failure? According to *Merriam-Webster*, the definition of *reproach* is an expression of rebuke or disapproval or to blame, discredit or disgrace. Do you any of those words describe how you feel about yourself at times? Self-reproach is basically not *accepting* and not *approving* of who you are, which is rejection of yourself.

When we are thinking thoughts of self-rejection and disapproval toward ourselves, we are setting ourselves up for failure. This type of thinking is toxic to the mind and to the body. The good news is that self-reproach can be healed and a healthier view of ourselves is possible. This chapter will humbly attempt to help you gain freedom from self-reproach.

SELF-REPROACH AND SICKNESS

When self-reproach and rejection are present in our lives, it as though there is a sign being held up that says: Cannot Heal until I Learn to Accept, Approve, and Love Myself—Faults and All. Feelings of self-reproach can suffocate and stifle our life. We pray to be healthy, we seek help from professionals, we take medication, and yet we see no change. Self-reproach is anger turned inward, which can lead to depression, anxiety, suicidal tendencies, and even physical illnesses. (I cover more on anxiety and depression in chapters 8 and 9.)

As I have said in earlier chapters, our body is listening to our thoughts and responding accordingly. The hypothalamus gland is the gland that connects the thoughts in our mind to our body.[1] When we experience negative emotions over long periods of time, especially negative emotions of self-rejection, our bodies respond. When we haven't learned to accept and love ourselves, this can show up as afflictions of the mind and body.

How do you see yourself?

I went to a conference where the speaker was rather shy and inexperienced, but what she had to say had a life changing impact on me. She talked about how we live with "self-fulfilling prophecies"; and what that means is that we live out what we believe about ourselves. We will never go beyond how we view ourselves. She began to ask us to really examine what we believed about ourselves.

I decided to go home and write on a sheet of paper all the positive qualities I believed about myself and all the negative qualities I believed about myself. The negative side was much longer, of course. The most interesting negative quality that I wrote down was that I believed I was a failure. I believed there were several areas in my life that I had failed at. I decided to look up the antonym or the opposite of the word *failure*; the opposite of a failure is *success*. I quickly realized that I would never become a success if I deep down saw myself as a failure. The Bible says, "As he thinks in his heart, so is he" (Prov. 23:7). I repented for thinking that way, and then I spent the next week declaring over myself that I am and will become a success. Within a short time, several important doors opened up for me. I would ask you to do the same thing. Make a list of the positive and negative qualities about yourself. Then take the negatives and look up their opposites. Begin to declare the opposites and the positive things over your life to counter the negative traits.

An example from King David

One morning in prayer God showed me a scripture that specifically says that self-reproach can lead to sickness. This portion of scripture comes from the psalms. It is a psalm of David when he was in a desperate place and he was pleading with the Lord for help.

It's important to understand a few things about King David. First, David's journey to becoming king was not an easy road. In fact, his own father passed him over as a candidate for king. The Bible tells us in 1 Samuel chapter 16, that the prophet Samuel was instructed by God to go to the house of Jesse (David's father) to choose the next king of Israel. God told Samuel He had provided Himself a king among Jesse's sons (v. 1). When the prophet Samuel arrived at Jesse's house, Samuel asked Jesse to show him his sons. Jesse brought out his sons, *except* David: "And Jesse made seven of his sons pass before Samuel" (v. 10).

Samuel looked each son over carefully waiting for God to say, this is the next king of Israel, but none of the sons were chosen by God (vv. 6–10). After observing all Jesse's sons, Samuel asked Jesse if he had any other sons. Jesse said, "There remains yet the youngest, and there he is, keeping the sheep" (v. 11). Jesses did not bring David out with the rest of his sons for Samuel to view. Why didn't Jesse to bring David out with the other brothers? Did Jesse not think that David was capable of being the next king of Israel? Did Jesse not have confidence that David could be a king? Apparently not, or Jesse would have brought David out!

When Samuel finally saw David, the Lord immediately spoke to Samuel and said concerning David, "Arise, anoint him; for this is the one!" (v. 12). The least likely son was the one God had chosen. This scripture passage teaches us that David's father did not have a lot of confidence in him to be king.

David's experience could be our experience. Have you ever had a parent or someone you respected communicate to you that they didn't see a lot of potential in you? Have you ever felt like you were unimportant or passed over? The good news is that even when others do not have confidence in us, God already knows the wonderful potential He put in us. In fact in 1 Samuel 16:7, we learn of the character of God:

> For the Lord does not see as man sees; for man looks at the outward appearance, but the Lord looks at the heart.

This was the beginning of David learning about the nature of God. If there was any emotion of reproach or shame in David, God was able to do the impossible in David's life and bring David to a place of confidence. David was not a sinless man, but he was a man who had a strong relationship with God. David is referred to as a man after God's own heart (Acts 13:22). This is encouraging to know that despite our shortcomings God can still move us forward.

This next scripture is the one I mentioned earlier, where the Bible teaches the connection between self-reproach and sickness. In Psalm 69 we get a glimpse of David talking to God.

> You know my reproach and my shame and my dishonor; All my adversaries are before You. *Reproach* has broken my heart and *I am so sick.*
> —Psalm 69:19–20, nas, emphasis added

This is an amazing insight into how feelings of self-reproach can negatively impact our health. Some translations translate the word *sickness* as *heaviness*; but the original Hebrew word means to be sick. This scripture says exactly what I had been experiencing—feelings of shame and reproach that led to sickness. For many years I felt like (I will quote directly from my diary of many years ago): "I must be the worst Christian, the worst wife, and the worst mother." If someone were to give me a compliment I would explain to them why the compliment did not apply. I felt disdain and disapproval toward myself. For decades I carried reproach. And just like the scripture says, "Reproach has broken my heart and I am so sick."

Notice that David says, "Reproach has broken my heart." When we have feelings of reproach against ourselves, our heart is broke because reproach says we are a failure and we can't do anything right. This has the potential to break our heart and lead to feelings of depression about ourselves and how we "turned out." This is not true of course; but when feelings of reproach are present in someone's life, they are basically rejecting themselves at the very core of who they are. Understand that the enemy of our souls entices us to wallow in these feelings. If we have the slightest propensity to feel reproach, he will sit on our shoulders and remind us of our shortcomings and past mistakes. Understand that this is the enemy's job but we are not powerless against him.

Opposite of Reproach is Approve, Honor, and Respect

What is the opposite of reproach? When I first researched the *opposite of reproach*, it was like a cold glass of water on a hot day. The opposite of reproach is to approve, honor, and respect. What? I'm supposed to approve, honor, and respect myself? Are you serious? Can we actually do that? This was such a foreign concept to me that I had to say this out loud to get my brain to agree. In fact, for about a month I would say it out loud: "I approve, honor, and respect myself." I would do this several times a day, until finally the words were no longer a surprise to me.

If you struggle in this area I would encourage you to do the same. Begin to say to yourself that you approve, honor and respect yourself. This is part of your healing, replacing the lie about yourself with the truth.

The Roots of Reproach

The reason why some people are more susceptible to reproach than others is because of past wounds in their life. Past circumstances or hurtful words have sent them a message saying, "You are not worthwhile; you are not important." These wounds have opened the door to reproach and opened the door to the enemy. These wounds can be healed, and the door can be shut to reproach and to the enemy.

There are many reasons for feeling self-reproach. I have listed common roots behind reproach that I have identified over the years. I will list them and then explain each root in greater detail.

1. Lack of encouragement and support from your family unit
2. Abandoned by a parent, spouse, or loved one
3. Not meeting expectations of someone or not measuring up
4. Verbal or physical abuse from a family member, spouse, or other person
5. Seemingly failed attempts at a career or goal
6. Committed a deed or crime for which you have never forgiven yourself

1. Lack of encouragement and support from family unit

Children crave the affection and approval that parents are supposed to provide for their children. If children do not receive these expressions of love, they begin to *look inward* and believe they are flawed. Parents or primary caregivers are the child's main source of love and significance. When parents spend time with their children and take care of their children, this sends a message to the child that he or she is valuable.

The opposite is also true. When the main caregiver of the child is too busy for the child or emotionally unavailable to the child, the child questions his or her significance. If the child does not receive love and acceptance, that child may grow up into adulthood with a low opinion of themselves because they did not first receive a healthy self-image at home. Sometimes parents are wrapped up in their own negativity or personal issues and they simply cannot give out what they don't have. Unfortunately, this can become a generational cycle that is passed down from one generation to the next.

A friend of mine experienced what it's like to grow up without either parent giving her value and significance. Her mother died when she was eight years old. Subsequently, not only did she not have her mother to give her value but her father was so distraught with grief that he was not able to give her the love and nurturing she needed. My friend spent many years battling insignificance and self-rejection. The more she found her identity in God, the more she was able to find her worth and value.

2. Abandoned by a parent, spouse, or loved one

The term "abandonment issues" has become synonymous with the pain and loss that comes when someone we love deeply leaves us. This loss could be the result of a divorce, a death, or a family member walking out. When someone is abandoned as a child or as an adult, this can open the door to feelings of self-reproach and self-rejection. The person who is abandoned concludes, "I must not be that valuable if they chose to leave me." They make the conclusion that they must not be loveable or significant because that loved one is gone. This can result in a person having a low opinion of themselves and not liking who they are. The unfortunate thing is that many adults have a belief that they are insignificant but they have never traced the root to a parent or loved one abandoning them.

I have already shared the experienced of having my father move halfway across the country and the battle I had with a broken heart. I didn't know that I would spend the next twenty years feeling like his decision to move was because something was wrong with me. One of my roots behind self-reproach is that I felt like I was not important enough for him to stay. The imprint that was left in my soul was that I must not be lovable or worth protecting because he left. I would later discover this was not the truth, but this was the lie that I lived under for many years. This opened the door for fear and insecurity to rule my life. These were lies that were deeply rooted within my soul.

The first step to healing was to recognize that this lie was part of my belief system. Once this lie was brought into the light, I then had to replace the lie with the truth. The truth is, I am lovable and I am worth protecting. I am worthwhile even though my father moved halfway across the country to pursue his life. Whether someone concludes that it is wrong or right for a parent to leave their child to pursue opportunities for a better life is up for debate. But what I do now know is that my father loved me despite his decision to move. In issues of abandonment it is important to realize that someone else's decision to leave does not mean we are flawed because they have left.

Divorce

Divorce can easily open the door to abandonment. Divorce affects so many families today that it's worth noting that children who come from divorced families may have a problem with self-rejection. I have talked with people who were not aware they were carrying self-blame and rejection from a divorce. It would be years later before they discovered they were carrying self-reproach because of their parents' divorce.

Divorce is so common today that many times this "root" of self-reproach goes unnoticed. Due to the commonality of divorce in our culture, many may conclude that the kids are alright, but the reality is; divorce can be devastating in a child's life *and the kids are not all right*. It may not be until the child grows up and has their own family that they realize how the divorce had a negative impact on them. Many children from divorced families grow up believing they did something wrong to cause the divorce, that somehow they are at fault for their family breaking up.

Children cannot evaluate why adults make decisions, rather they see the parents' split as a direct reflection on them. They conclude the divorce must be their fault and they are somehow to blame. As the child grows up, these feelings get buried and the person still displays a poor self-image, not realizing that one of the roots maybe from the divorce. I am not saying that all people who experienced divorce as a child suffer from self-rejection; I am saying it is a possible root to a fruit of self-rejection.

When a spouse leaves

Being abandoned by a spouse, particularly in the case of adultery, can devastate a person's self-image. They may have thoughts such as, "I must not have been good enough because they found someone else," or, "If only I was more desirable to my partner," or, "If could have made them happier then maybe they wouldn't have left." Feelings of low self-worth and an inability to please their partner can leave a huge dent in their self-worth.

When a spouse leaves, it does not mean there is something wrong with the remaining spouse. It's important to separate the leaving spouse's issues with the remaining spouse's value. It may take some time and counseling to work through the grief of a spouse leaving, but in the end God does not want the person to have an imprint of self-rejection because their spouse left.

3. Not meeting expectations of someone or not measuring up

This is another setup for low self-worth. For those of us who struggle with perfectionism, we wrestle with not feeling good enough because we have to be perfect first. I remember going to my favorite cousin's house when I was a young girl. My cousin, who was about my age, was asked by her mother to put the silverware away in a drawer. She didn't want to do this simple task for her mother. But I remember thinking that if I did this chore and did it perfectly, her mother would be pleased with me. I was about nine at the time. I was seeking approval and value by trying to do something perfectly. There was a hole of self-reproach in my life and I was trying to fill it will with trying to be perfect.

Eventually I would learn that worth is not based on how good we do a task but by the fact that God chose to create us. The truth is that God is the One who places value on us, not on how perfect we attempt to be for others.

Sometimes people do not feel good about themselves because a sibling or friend always shined and they felt like they were in the shadows. Perhaps the "other" person had the better home life, better house, better clothes, etc., and this left them feeling less than, like they were not good enough. Comparing ourselves to others and striving to feel "good enough" can take the very life out of us. We knock ourselves out trying to prove our worth and measure up to those around us. This is an extremely toxic way to live that can also lead to illness.

4. Verbal or physical abuse from a family member, spouse, or other person

Verbal abuse

Words are extremely powerful, and they can leave a trail of hurt and devastation in our life. As you're reading this right now, you can probably recall a time when someone you love said something that pierced your heart and wounded you. Even if they were not necessarily verbally abusive, their words still haunt you today.

When someone uses their words to devalue us or make us feel like we are not valuable, this can open the door to a root of self-rejection. If our parents or someone we look up to tells us that they don't see potential in us, then we surmise we are inferior.

I knew a woman who always felt like a failure athletically. All through high school she was very self-conscious feeling like a klutz. She wouldn't dare go out for a sport. Years later she told me that growing up her father always told her that she wasn't very good athletically. She believed this and accepted this, and her self-image was shaped by his words. It wasn't until later in her life that she discovered she enjoyed volleyball and other fun sports and also discovered she was good at those sports. Her father's words shaped how she viewed herself and had a negative impact on her.

Verbal abuse takes the occasional harmful word and turns it up a notch. Continual hurtful words shame us and devalue us. Verbal abuse is that constant criticism that can cause emotional scars. The power and pain of those words can be healed by grieving over those words, recognizing they are not true about you, forgiving the person, and finally by releasing those words to God.

Word curses

Words spoken that negatively impact our life are referred to as "word curses." When someone speaks negatively over your life and it shapes your future and shapes the course of your life, this is a word curse. This curse can be reversed. If you're living under negative words spoken by someone else or even negative words spoken by yourself, the impact of those words can cease to torment your life. And I'm going to tell you how!

I have personally experienced God reversing word curses. A doctor once told me that I was going to be sick with a virus for six years. At first I was devastated at this news. Since he was a doctor, I thought he was right. He was wrong. I had to come out of agreement with the word curse he spoke over my life, and I had to come into agreement with what God says about my situation. I had to renew my mind with God's words of healing found in the Bible. I had to determine that the doctor did not have the final say over my life, but God has the final say over my life. I had to find scriptures that were the opposite of the doctor's words, and I had to declare those scriptures over my life. My faith in God had the final say, and it did not take me six years to recover.

To reverse a word curse that either someone has spoken over your life or that you have spoken over your own life, you can first begin to come out of agreement with those words that were spoken over you. Secondly, say the prayer below and mean it with all your heart. Thirdly, find scriptures that are the opposite of that word curse. And the fourth step is to daily declare over your life what God says about you. It may take a few days to a few months of declaring out loud God's truth over your life, but that word curse will be broken. You see, the only way negative words curse your life is when you believe those words. That's why it's so important to come out of agreement with those words.

> *God, please forgive* _____ *(person's name or yourself) for saying those words over my life. In the name of Jesus, I cancel the effects and the power of*

those words. God help me to live Your plan for my life and reverse all curses that have been spoken against me. I cover those words with the shed blood of Jesus Christ. I recognize that Jesus Christ died on the cross to set me free from all curses. Lord, I now come out of agreement with all negative, hurtful words and I come into agreement with Your words (the Bible) over my life. I pray in the name of Your Son Jesus. Amen.

Isaiah 54:17 says, "No weapon formed against you shall prosper, And every tongue which rises against you in judgment, You shall be condemn. This is the heritage of the servants of the Lord." When we have a relationship with Jesus Christ, we are under His protection; and as long as we refuse to come into agreement with another person's words, we can be free of word curses.

Physical abuse

Physical abuse can also affect self-image. In physical abuse cases, the victim may feel flawed or damaged as a result of the abuse. The abuse can open the door to feelings of low self-worth and feelings of self-reproach. The victim will need time to work through the negative feelings that are associated with the abuse. Grieving over the abuse and finding forgiveness for their abuser will be important to move beyond self-reproach and other damaging emotions. Christian counseling or the support of a good friend to work through the lies they may now believe about themselves may be necessary. The good news is that there are countless success stories of people who have overcome the negative self-image that was the result of their abuse.

5. Seemingly failed attempt at career or goals

When we think we have failed at a career, goal, job, or even a relationship, this can be a huge blow to our self-image and open the door for a root of self-reproach to grow. Whatever that perceived failure is, it's toxic to walk under the umbrella of such statements as, "I keep failing at everything I try and do."

Several years ago I started a cheesecake business. Baking is a hobby of mine, and I thought this could be a good career for me. I worked hard to start the business. I got all the state licenses that were necessary and went through all the red tape that is required to start a business. I was able to sell my cheesecakes in a dozen grocery stores. The problem was that I was working very hard but making little to no profit. I continued on with the business to see if I would eventually be "successful." I wasn't. I had to make the tough decision to close the business. When I closed the business down I felt like a terrible failure. I told my husband, see I failed *again* at something.

I smile now when I look back at that season of my life. I'm so thankful that the little cheesecake business didn't make it. If it would have worked out I wouldn't be fulfilling my purpose—to help people who are stuck in emotional and physical afflictions. I get more joy out of helping others than I do baking cheesecakes. I still bake and I still enjoy baking, but I know it's not my purpose. God knew what was going to make me truly fulfilled in life; and He has a way of opening and closing the appropriate doors.

We can look at our past and we can learn what *not* to do. Let's change our dialogue around concerning our perceived failures. Instead of, "I've failed," we could say, "That door is shut for me." Instead of, "I can't do anything right," we could say, "I've learned what is not a good fit for me.

Perceived failure is really a teacher. Next time you're tempted to get down on yourself for an area in your life that didn't work out, look at what can be learned from that experience. Recognize that God may have a different path (more fulfilling) for you to take!

6. Committed a deed or crime for which you have never forgiven yourself

This root damages our self-worth because of a wrong deed that we committed against others or ourselves. This wrong deed could be something we said or did or something we were involved in that we shouldn't have been. We may feel like we don't deserve to feel good about ourselves because of the past mistake.

I remember a time when I said something that was completely out of line. As soon as the words came out of my mouth, I knew I was wrong. I criticized myself for weeks for what I said, and I felt like a terrible person. I told everyone how bad I was and what an awful mistake I made. I finally got so tired of feeling bad about myself that I went to the cross, fell on my knees, and asked God to forgive me. I made the decision to never make that same mistake again. I needed to get out of self-hate for what I did and get back into God's grace and mercy.

There comes a point when we accept the wrong that we did, receive God's forgiveness, have mercy on ourselves, and move on. The definition of *mercy*, according to *Merriam-Webster*, is "compassion or forbearance shown especially to an offender." When we have offended, we can go to the cross and find mercy for our circumstance. Jesus died a horrible death on the cross so that our sins can be forgiven. We can let go of that root of self-reproach regardless of our past mistakes!

If you have experienced any one of the above six causes for reproach, there is a good chance the enemy has found an open door to torment you with self-rejection. The enemy of our soul looks for an opportunity into our lives. The six possible roots that I have presented are not all-inclusive. There may be other roots to self-rejection, but it's worth spending some time in prayer asking God if any of these apply to you. The companion workbook (available at www.luanndunnuck.com) is a great tool to be able to do this.

Approval Addiction

I would be amiss if I did not address approval addiction. Approval addiction is the continual need of the approval of others to feel good about who you are. The approval-addicted person is trying to get the attention of people who are in a *position of authority* or *a person who carries influence* to notice them. People who fall into this category go the extra mile to get these people to **praise** and recognize them.

Many times approval-addicted people go beyond their physical and emotional limitations to show others their strengths. The need to be recognized is so strong that they choose careers they don't like, say yes to things they wished they said no to, and give of themselves when they have nothing left to give. The most insecure of us are the busiest and hardest workers, and the most "driven" among us can be the shakiest when it comes to having confidence. This is all for the sake of having that "important" person notice them. Approval addiction is exhausting, depletes us of our energy, and can lead to physical and emotional illness.

I do want to mention that there is nothing wrong with a boss or person in authority giving you a compliment, but it gets out of balance when your day does not go right unless you're recognized by that important person.

To begin to get free from approval addiction, the first step is to recognize that you are someone who struggles in this area. You cannot confront what you are in denial of. Once I recognized that I was making decisions based on trying to get the approval of others, I was grieved. I was grieved because I was inadvertently letting other people's opinions guide my life. To put this in Bible terms, I was making an idol out of the approval of others. I was trying to please people more than I was trying to please God.

To put an end to approval addiction, it's important to seek God for our self-worth and not others. This is when I realized I had to get my worth from the Word of God. I went on a mission to learn how God sees me.

At the end of this chapter, I have provided scriptures that will enable you to see your value from God's eyes. A principle that I advocate throughout this book is to acquire scriptures that replace the lies with the truth.

In this case, the lies we have lived under are that we are not important, we are insignificant, and we are not as good as others. And because of this type of thinking, we hunger for the approval of others. This is where it's important to retrain how we view ourselves based on the words of God. Someone once said that the root behind addictions is the need to be loved. This statement holds true when it comes to approval addiction. If we truly knew that we are deeply loved by God and we liked ourselves, faults and all, we would not need the approval of others. That is the truth.

Another important step to take to get free from approval addiction is to check your *motives*. Ask yourself *why* you are committing to that organization, why you are volunteering for that project. Why are you signing up for that committee? Is it because you want to be helpful and pursue that path, or are you doing it to be recognized by others? Checking our motives is important because we want to move in the direction God has for us rather than the direction that pleases others.

A side note to parents: we need to make sure we are not putting pressure on our children to pursue a career or path that *we* would prefer. We need to make sure they are not following our career choice because they are trying to get our approval. We don't want our children to choose a direction in life that pleases us rather we want them to follow God's plan for their lives.

Breaking free from approval addiction is a process. Like any addiction, it is a habit that we have lived with for so long, it will take time to change our thinking. Examining the "roots" behind self-rejection will also help to understand why we have such a strong need for approval from others. Once we get to the root of "why" we struggle with self-rejection, we will find that we no longer have a strong need to get our significance from other people.

I no longer need the approval of others to feel worthwhile. I like who I am—faults and all. This is very freeing! We all have strengths and weaknesses; and we work on our weaknesses. But the fact that we have weaknesses doesn't mean we are invaluable. Everyone has areas of struggle. No one is perfect.

I encourage you to drop the weight of thinking you're unlovable and insignificant because of your struggles. God put you on this earth because He loves you and because He has a good plan for your life (Jer. 29:11) *that only you can fulfill.* You are unique in who you are. Ultimately we aim to please God and not man. A pat on the back from God far out weights a compliment or recognition from man.

IDENTITY QUESTION

Recently I was asked the question, "Where do you get your identity?" This is a great question; because unless we know who we are, we will have difficulty accepting ourselves. Do we get our identity from our jobs, what we own, who we know, or from our accomplishments? To receive our identity based on the above criteria will only create an unstable foundation for our lives. Our true identity is found in God and what He says about us. We don't want to be dependent on public opinion, our jobs, or our accomplishments to feel worthwhile. If we get our identity from worldly achievements or what others think of us, we will be on a continual roller-coaster ride of instability.

We want to heal from feelings of insecurity and reproach; and in order to do that, we need to know exactly who we are. I thought about all the scriptures that

I could find to show worth and value (and if you struggle in this area; you should be familiar with God's words about your identity).

But if I had to sum up our identity, I would sum it up with four words: I am God's daughter, or I am God's son. Period! I am His child and God is my Father. God is a good Father who knows how to care for His child. This is the basis for our identity. Our identity is not based on our past, our achievements, or others' opinion of us. We are His child, and no one can take that status away from us!

Everyone can be celebrated in three areas: (1) we are made in the image of God, (2) we carry gifts given by God to be used for His glory, and (3) we can carry the presence of the Holy Spirit.

The first step in healing from self-rejection and reproach is to know your identity. Once you know your identity, then you can refute the enemy when he comes to remind you of your past mistakes or your weaknesses. You can remind him that you are God's child and fully accepted by Him. When you know that you are accepted by God, faults and all, then you can accept yourself.

I remember saying to God, "Have You looked at my resume lately? It's not very good. Are You sure You want to work through me?" If you examine the people in the Bible that God used, you will find that many of them did not have the credentials one might expect. Nonetheless, God sees past our weaknesses and He sees our potential!

Jesus' Resurrection

We can understand God's love and value to us in two ways: (1) through Jesus' death and resurrection, and (2) through God's love letter to us, the Bible.

God sent His *only* Son to die for you. Think about that truth for a moment. Imagine if you had to give up your only beloved child for the sake of someone else. That is what God did for you. He exchanged His Son's life for yours. You are of such tremendous value that God sent His Son to die a horrible death just because He thought you are worth it.

Not only did Jesus experience a cruel death, but the Bible also says that Jesus conquered death, hell, and the grave. What does that mean exactly? Jesus kicked the devil's butt and took away his authority all for humanity. You and I are that important to God. God sent Jesus to redeem our lives from all the hurt and pain we have ever suffered and ever will suffer. When we think about how much God loves us, there is no room for self-rejection. God calls us acceptable, and for us to call ourselves unacceptable is to disagree with God.

The Written Word

Fathers play a crucial role in the development of both boys and girls. It's the father who shapes the boy into a man, and it is the father's presence in a little girl's life that will tell her she is beautiful and worthwhile. If you had a strong father figure in your life, that is a wonderful blessing. But if you did not, starting today, God wants to be that strong Father figure in your life. If you are a man, He wants to be the One who tells you that you have what it takes and you can conquer whatever comes your way. If you are woman, God wants to tell you He thinks you are lovely and beautiful and He created you with potential and promise. God's love for us is not conditional on our behavior. He will not take His love away from us when we fail or make a mistake. God is love and He thinks you're important enough to have been born on this earth to fulfill the assignment that He has given you. God has a tender message of hope and affection for you. If you have been wounded by others devaluing you, God wants to show you your value found in His Word.

Take a few moments and read the scriptures below and let these truths sink deep into your soul. When I was healing from self-reproach, I had to put theses scriptures on my refrigerator or on my mirror in my bathroom and read them until my heart healed from self-rejection and my thinking changed. Our minds need to be renewed according to His Word and not our past experiences. I would eventually see myself as God sees me. This is an important step in shutting the door to self-reproach in your life. After each of the scriptures below, I have sentences contrasting what God says about us with some possible negative replies that we may respond with. As you read, ask yourself which you believe—God's promise to you or the negative words.

> He kept [me] as the apple of His eye.
> —Deuteronomy 32:10

- God says: You are My princess or My beloved son.
- We say: No one has treated me like a beautiful princess or a beloved son. I must be no good to God or anyone else.

> I am fearfully and wonderfully made; Marvelous are [His] works [me].
> —Psalm 139

- God says: You are beautifully and wonderfully created; you are His workmanship.
- We say: I am permanently flawed; and because of my flaws I am unlovable and unacceptable.

[I am] complete in Him.
—Colossians 2:10

- God says: He made me complete in Christ.
- We say: I will never be complete because of all the things I have done wrong.

He chose [me] in Him before the foundation of the world, that [I] should be holy and without blame before Him in love.
—Ephesians 1:4

- God says: He chose me and I am without blame because of the cross of Jesus Christ.
- We say: I feel reproach and self-rejection because of my faults and mistakes.

[I am] chosen of God, holy and beloved.
—Colossians 3:12, nas

- God says: He chose me and dearly loves me.
- I say: I am unlovable because I have not been told or shown affection that let me know I am loved.

[I] have redemption through His blood, the forgiveness of sins.
—Colossians 1:14

- God says: My past, current, and future sins are and will be forgiven if I bring them to the cross.
- We say: My sins are too great to ever forgive, and I will probably never change; therefore, God will never truly accept me.

If you agreed with any of the negative replies from the above statements, then you are not agreeing with God about who you are. Our thinking should line up with God's scriptures. The goal is to *not* be in direct opposition to what God says about us. We don't want to devalue ourselves any longer. God is the Creator. He is the One who breathed life into you. He thinks you are the best thing since chocolate ice cream. Life may have tarnished you or beat you down, or perhaps your own choices may have blemished you; but God wants to free you. He desires to redeem and bring fulfillment to your life.

My self-reproach and self-rejection were evidence that I was cursing myself. I was in disobedience to God by my self-reproach. I needed to confess to God that I would begin to love and accept myself despite my weaknesses and flaws. We open ourselves up to emotional or physical curses when we come into agreement with the devil about who we are. We are not to curse what He had blessed; and He has blessed you and He had blessed me.

In Conclusion

If or when the devil attempts to devalue you, you will be equipped with the Word of God to refute the devil. You will be armed with the Word of God to fend off any attack the devil may wage on your identity. You no longer have to define yourself by reproach and rejection! Below is a prayer followed by declarations from scripture to help you further understand how God sees you. If any of the listed scriptures jump off the page to you, you may want to write them out and put them in a place where you can read them every day. You, my friend, are God's beloved and treasured child.

Prayer

God, I pray You would help me to recognize when rejection tries to steal my peace and rob my identity that is found in You. Continue to teach me how to use Your Word to defeat the lies of rejection. Help me to see that I am worthwhile and valuable in Your eyes. I accept the truth that I don't need the approval of others to like who I am. I stand not in my own righteousness but in the righteousness of Jesus Christ. Holy Spirit, wrap me in the truth that I am loved and cherished by You. Grant me the grace to love myself, including my strengths and weaknesses. I will meditate on Your love letter to me, the Bible. In Jesus' name I pray. Amen.

- I am a child of God (John 1:12).
- I am a son (daughter) of God; God is spiritually my father (Rom. 8:14–15; Gal. 3:26).
- I am a temple of God. His Spirit and His life dwell in me (1 Cor. 3:16, 6:19).
- I am a new creation (2 Cor. 5:17).
- I am a fellow citizen with the rest of God's family (Eph. 2:19).
- I am a citizen of heaven (Phil. 3:20; Eph. 2:6).
- I am hidden in Christ with God (Col. 3:3).
- I am a son or daughter of light and not of darkness (1 Thess. 5:5).

- I am one of God's living stones, being built up in Christ as a spiritual house (1 Pet. 2:5).
- I am a member of a chosen race, a royal priesthood, a holy nation, a people for God's own possession (1 Pet. 2:9–10).
- I have been alive together with Christ (Eph. 2:5).
- I have direct access to God through the Spirit (Eph. 2:18).
- I have been rescued from the dominion of Satan's rule and transferred to the kingdom of Christ (Col. 1:13).
- I have been given a spirit of power, love, and a sound mind (2 Tim. 1:7)
- I am born of God, and the evil one the devil cannot touch me (1 John. 5:18)
- I have been placed into Christ by God's doing (1 Cor. 1:30).
- I have been given the mind of Christ (1 Cor. 2:16).
- I have been established, anointed, and sealed by God in Christ (2 Cor. 1:21).
- I have been given the Holy Spirit as a pledge guaranteeing my inheritance to come (Eph. 1:14).

Chapter 7
GUILT AND ACCUSATION

*L*IVING WITH GUILT is like living with a fifty-pound bag of potatoes strapped to your back. The load of guilt is a very heavy one that comes to steal our emotional and physical health. There is a strong connection between guilt, and self-reproach; because once we feel guilty over something, then we tend to get mad at ourselves, thus falling into self-reproach and self-loathing. This is a tormenting cycle of guilt and self-reproach in which many are stuck. There is a way out.

GUILT AND SICKNESS

Guilt is extremely destructive. In fact, some people will remain sick as a way to punish themselves for their wrongdoings or *perceived* wrongdoings. As I have studied this subject and personally lived it, I have found that guilt hinders the immune system and the body's ability to heal. Below is a summary of an article by *BBC News*, April 16, 2000, "Guilt 'Bad for Your Health,'" which shows the harmful effects of guilt on the immune system:

> [The article] reports the results of a study that indicates that people who felt guilty had lower levels of immunoglobulin A. High levels of immunoglobulin A are associated with a strong immune system, and the ability to fight off illness. The researcher's previous studies showed that people with low levels of guilt were less likely to go to the doctor, or to report suffering from colds or flu.[1]

This study found that people who have guilt have *low* levels of immunoglobulin A. Immunoglobulin A is one of five categories of immunoglobulins, also known as antibodies. Antibodies are made by the body's immune system to fight off bacteria, viruses, fungus, and cancer cells. The purpose of the antibody is to attack foreign invaders, destroy them, thus protecting our health.[2]

The above study shows the parallel between guilt and low levels of antibodies or a decrease in immune function. People with guilt have a lower amount of these antibodies to fight off disease and infections; guilt lowers the immune system. God put the immune system in place to fight off a variety of diseases and maladies.

Guilt says to the body *and the mind*, "You don't deserve to be well for what you have done; you don't deserve anything good to come your way; you deserve punishment for your mistakes." As a side note, false guilt can produce the same effect in the body.

We are going to be discussing guilt and false guilt. There is a difference between the two, and it's important to identify which one is operating in our life. We will first address the issue of false guilt.

FALSE GUILT

False guilt is an unnecessary burden that a lot of us carry. False guilt probably plagues more people than actual guilt. Some of us have lived with false guilt for so long that it is indiscernible to us. I have listed below four descriptions of false guilt. Thoroughly read the definitions and see if you can identify with one or more of the definitions.

It is my prayer that the Holy Spirit will illuminate the destructive root of false guilt in your life. There was one area of false guilt in my life that I didn't recognize until I was helping a friend work through her false guilt. When I finished helping her, it was like looking in a mirror. May the definitions below be your mirror. Carefully observe the descriptions below and see if you can relate.

False Guilt is when you are:

1. **Feeling blame over a circumstance that was beyond your control.** There may have been extenuating circumstances that you could do nothing about, yet you still feel guilty. You could not intervene or change the situation, but the guilt still plagues you.

2. **Feeling guilty because you think you are not doing enough to help someone when you have no more emotional or physical resources left to help that person.** Guilt nags at you because you believe you should continue to aid this person, but if you continued to help this person you or your family may suffer.

3. **Feeling guilty for a situation in which you committed no wrong deed.** Your intentions were good, yet you were misunderstood and you were blamed for something you did not do.

4. **The scapegoat for others:** *Merriam-Webster* says a *scapegoat* is, "one that bears the blame for others; one that is the object of irrational hostility." When someone can't handle their own negative, miserable life, they blame you for their circumstances.

    I remember when I was a child our beloved family dog was hit by a car and died. Because I happened to be the one that let the dog out that evening, a family member came down hard on me and blamed me for the death of the dog. This is an example of being the scapegoat.

Do you see yourself in any of these four scenarios? Did any of the descriptions jump off the page to you? The first step in healing false guilt is to recognize your area of brokenness and frustration. Sometimes we become so accustomed to carrying false guilt that we have no idea it's harming us. We will get to the steps to take to heal from false guilt at the end of our discussion.

Personal examples of false guilt

I have realized at various times in my life that I was carrying false guilt without knowing it. There were some situations for which I carried false guilt for decades and didn't realize it until God pointed those areas out.

Something beyond my control

The first example I'm going to share with you involves a situation in my life where I had *no control* over the circumstances, yet I still felt guilty. This example is from my childhood:

When I was first married, I was experiencing severe panic attacks. I was trying to read everything I could to figure out what was wrong with me. I remember reading a Christian self-help book; as I was reading a certain paragraph, two words seem to jump off the page at me: NOT GUILTY. I kept reading those words over and over again, thinking, "Why are these words jumping off the page at me?" Every time I said those words out loud, it was though a healing balm was going through my mind and body.

As I was saying those words over and over, "Not Guilty, not guilty," a memory from my childhood flashed before my eyes. This memory was of my mother being physically abused and hit by her former husband.

In an instant it all made sense to me: God was showing me that I had carried false guilt because *I could not protect my mother* from this man. *As a young child I felt that I failed to keep my mother safe.* I was only eleven at the time, yet as a child I felt a sense of responsibility to protect her.

Now, as an adult looking back, I recognize that an eleven-year-old child is powerless over the actions of a grown man. But that day God showed me the false guilt that I had been carrying for decades. I unnecessarily felt guilty because my mother was abused and I could do nothing to stop it. When God showed that to me, I was able to pray and ask God to pull that root of false guilt out of my heart and heal that wound. The simple act of God showing me that memory of the false guilt that was buried deep within my soul gave me a level of healing.

It was as though God was removing a splinter from my heart that day, and there would be many more splinters He would remove. The Holy Spirit is the best Counselor and the best splinter remover. He has the wisdom and knows the correct timing to show us what hinders us.

Committing no wrong

Another example of false guilt is a more recent experience where I was tempted to come under false guilt. A friend, who has battled insecurity, saw me involved with an event that was producing positive results. She communicated to me in a "joking" way that she *should* have been a part of this event. I recognized she was being tempted to get angry *with me* because *I was invited* to be part of an event and she wasn't and this bothered her.

She gave me the cold shoulder for a period of time. I could feel her distancing herself from me and *I started to feel guilty*. I knew she was upset because she was not a part of this event. I thought perhaps I should call her and ask if I had done anything to offend her. Then I very quickly said to myself, "Wait a minute I feel like I am being manipulated to feel guilty."

The irony here is that she was upset with me because I walked through a door God opened for me. She was giving me the cold shoulder because she was not invited to walk through that same door.

I came to my senses, and said, "I am not going to go to her like a guilty lamb and try and convince her to stop being mad at me." I simply prayed God would encourage her and help her to feel secure and worthwhile in her own path that God chose for her. Eventually she got over it and would later admit that she was being childish. The friendship was restored and we were able to move past this incident. But do you see how we can be manipulated to feel guilty because of someone else's insecurities?

Manipulated by a family member

The final example of false guilt is an area that I carried all my life, until recently, and didn't even know it. I taught on false guilt, I knew what it was, and I was trying to keep myself free from it; but one day the Lord took blinders off my eyes.

I saw the harm that false guilt produced in my life like never before when a friend that I was trying to comfort called to tell me of her situation. The situation was that a close family member of hers called to ask her if she would leave her home and move in with them to take care of them. The family member offered to pay her to do all of this. The problem was that my friend would have to move to another state, leave a stable job, and leave her adult children and grandkids and everything that was familiar to her.

My friend began to feel *extremely* guilty because she didn't want to move, yet she wanted to honor this family member's request for help. There were other options for this family member to get the help they needed. Yet, because the family member asked *her* and this was a *close family member*, my friend felt guilty. My friend was struggling with *a tremendous sense of obligation* to make this move. After wrestling with this for a period of time she made the decision not to move. The guilt she was wrestling with subsided after she made the decision. She was able to find her peace in understanding God's direction for her life.

After I hung up the phone with this friend, it occurred to me that what she just described is what a certain family member of mine had done to me most of my life and was still doing. I never recognized the amount of manipulation and control this family member had over me until I was helping someone else in a similar situation.

I will tell you that initially I became angry at this family member for all the times they leaned on me and took my strength, especially in times when I had little strength to give. I knew that I needed to *stop feeling sorry* for this person and give them over to God. I let myself grieve over this situation and eventually I forgave them. Going forward I was very aware to not fall into the trap of false guilt with this person.

The first step toward changing this toxic relationship was to recognize it was hurting me and then making decisions that were led by the Holy Spirit. We cannot heal from something we aren't aware of.

Prayer for False Guilt

You may want to take a few moments now and ask God to reveal to you if you have false guilt over a situation in your life. If you find that you *have* carried false guilt over a situation, you may want to say the prayer below, *to begin the process* of freeing your soul from this burden.

> *Holy Spirit, I ask You to take the blinders off my eyes and show me hidden areas where I have come under false guilt. Holy Spirit, heal any sickness in my body, soul, or spirit that is the result of false guilt. Remove from my life all toxic effects of carrying this burden. Grant me the wisdom to know when false guilt is trying to get a foothold in my life. Holy Spirit, thank You for Your healing and cleansing power. In Jesus' name I pray. Amen.*

You may want to spend some time talking with a good friend or journaling about areas of your life where you feel you have come under false guilt. Once you recognize that you don't have to feel guilty, you will find it easier to live free in this area.

Guilt

We will now move to the second part of our discussion: guilt that is the result of our past mistakes. This type of guilt *and condemnation* attempts to take our past and hold us hostage.

It should be noted that there is a difference between guilt and conviction. Conviction is that gentle tap on the shoulder from the Holy Spirit that lets us know when have done something wrong or when we are about to do something wrong. When we sin or make a mistake the Holy Spirit leads us to repentance and helps us turn from our mistakes. The Holy Spirit leads us into godly ways of thinking which produces godly living. When we sin, we repent to God and ask for forgiveness. Then, with the help of the Holy Spirit, we turn from our wrongdoing. This is the conviction from the Holy Spirit and this is a healthy way to live. If we have to go to another person and confess our mistake and make our wrong right then we should do that to. But after we have repented to God and others, then we need to let it go.

I want to address the issue of when we can't seem to let our past mistakes go and we continually feel guilty.

The compassion of God

I can be sensitive to feeling guilty if I feel like I have hurt someone's feelings or if I feel like I have disobeyed God. If I have done either, I know I need to make my wrong right.

I'm grateful that over the years I have come to understand that God is not a harsh God who is constantly angry with us. I have come to understand that God looks at the heart of a person and He understands the *why* behind our wrong choices. God knows if we have sinned because of an old wound or an abuse or if we committed the sin out of insecurities, pride, or selfishness. God can see if we are truly repentant for our wrongdoing, or if we are callous and hard-hearted toward our sin.

What is the heart of God in circumstances where we are still mad at ourselves for our past mistakes? In order to stop feeling guilt over our past, it's important to know what God would say to us concerning our wrongdoings. The best illustration of this is found in the Gospel of John. This is the account of the women caught in the act of adultery. In this account everyone knew the woman's sin. Her peers were ready to stone her because of her actions. But Jesus had an entirely different view of this woman who was shamed and humiliated.

> Then the scribes and Pharisees brought to Him a woman caught in adultery. And when they had set her in the midst, they said to Him,

> "Teacher, this woman was caught in adultery, in the very act. Now Moses, in the law, commanded us that such should be stoned. But what do You say?" This they said, testing Him, that they might have something of which to accuse Him. But Jesus stooped down and wrote on the ground with His finger, as though He did not hear. So when they continued asking Him, He raised Himself up and said to them, "He who is without sin among you, let him throw a stone at her first." And again He stooped down and wrote on the ground. Then those who heard it, being convicted by their conscience, went out one by one, beginning with the oldest even to the last. And Jesus was left alone, and the woman standing in the midst. When Jesus had raised Himself up and saw no one but the woman, He said to her, "Woman, where are those accusers of yours? Has no one condemned you?" She said, "No one, Lord." And Jesus said to her, "Neither do I condemn you; go and sin no more."
>
> —John 8:3–11

Can you catch a glimpse of the heart of God here? Notice how Jesus ministers to this woman who was caught in the act of adultery. He doesn't respond to her with accusation and blame; He doesn't even condemn her. He very easily could have made her feel shamed and guilty, but He chose not to. Instead, Jesus is very gentle in His dealings with her. He simply instructs her to stop participating in her sin.

Jesus said to her, "Neither do I condemn you." He was saying to her, "*I'm absolving you* of your wrongdoings; *I'm freeing you* of your sins." Can you sense His tenderness with her? Can you observe the gentle way He speaks to her? Jesus is not harsh or condemning. He addresses her in the opposite manner of how her accusers treated her.

The Holy Spirit is gently saying to you, it's time to let it go. It's time to leave your mistakes in the past. Your slate is clean.

ACCUSATIONS

We cannot discuss guilt without talking about accusations. Accusation is the glue that keeps guilt and self-reproach intact. We are going to look at three areas of accusation, (1) when the devil brings accusation against us, (2) when others bring accusation against us (understand that the enemy can use people to bring accusation against us), and (3) when we accuse ourselves.

Living under accusations can make letting our mistakes go more difficult. Most of us try really hard not to get involved with things we will regret later, but occasionally we make mistakes. We know when we've messed up and usually we are remorseful for our actions or words. The very last thing we need is someone accusing us of our already regretful past.

To *accuse* means to charge with a fault or to blame. We are the first one to recognize our mistake; but to be accused adds more pain to our already broken spirit. Accusations or *perceived* accusations can keep us stuck in guilt. Perceived accusation is when we think that someone is accusing us or judging us, when in actuality they are not. Some of us are sensitive to feeling guilty, and we can easily assume others are judging us. It's important to know whether we are being accused by others or if we are *assuming* we are being accused. Either real accusation or perceived accusation can keep us stuck in guilt.

Three areas of accusation

1. When the enemy accuses us

Picture the cartoon where devil sits on a person's shoulder and speaks to them. The devil attempts to hurl accusations at us which keep guilt intact in our lives. The Bible refers to the devil as the "accuser of the brethren." In Revelation chapter 12, verse 10, it says, "The accuser of our brethren, who accused [us] before our God day and night."

When we make a mistake, the devil seizes the moment and takes advantage of our mistakes by tempting us to feel shamed and condemned. The enemy looks for opportunities to accuse us, because he knows accusation will keep us stuck in guilt. He knows that as long as we are reminded of our past and *all* the mistakes we've ever made, the cycle of guilt and self-rejection will continue. He knows better than we do that this cycle can open us up to emotional and physical sickness.

His goal is for us to live in regret, somehow wishing we could go back and make different choices. This of course is unrealistic. We cannot go back and change things. As I mentioned earlier, the enemy sits on our shoulder and presents condemning thoughts as though those thoughts were our own. We take those thoughts and accept them, and we begin to come into agreement with the devil. The devil's lies become our truths. This is deception. When he throws those guilty thoughts our way, we begin to feel horrible about ourselves and this can lead to self-reproach and sickness.

We fall prey to the idea that what we did was so bad that it is unforgivable. This is where the cross of Jesus Christ can become our *defense* against the devil's accusations. The way to get free from this type of accusations is to first recognize that the regretful, guilty thoughts are coming from the enemy. He is throwing those thoughts our way to see if we will accept his bait. After reading this, when you feel yourself going down that road of feeling guilty for your past hold up that mental stop sign and say, "No!"

The good news of the gospel is that Jesus Christ, who is fully God, came to this earth to take away our sins. We can stand up to those condemning accusations by reminding the devil that our past *is forgivable*. Remind the devil that because of the cross of Jesus Christ our past is forgiven. Jesus suffered and died so that you and I could live free from the burden of our sins. We do not have to live under the heavy load of guilt, and we do not have to live under the devil's lies about our life. We can exchange *our guilt* for Jesus' work on the cross.

We are replacing lies with truth. The key here is that we need to know the truth to be able to get free of guilt. The truth is we are free to be loved and accepted by God and we are free to love and accept ourselves. When I began to live this way I found freedom from the constant nagging feeling of guilt.

What does the Bible say about our sins, mistakes, and wrong choices? I have listed below a few scriptures that counter the idea that our sins are unforgivable. The best way to get God's truths planted in our heart is to say a scripture out loud that specifically addresses the issue of guilt.

Research shows that we are more likely to believe what we hear out of our own mouth. If you struggle with guilt, read these scriptures and let truth wash over you. You may want to post some of these scriptures around your house (I have done this for years and it is the best way to get scripture into your soul).

These scriptures counteract the years of guilt you've been living under with God's message of redemption. You are creating healthy thoughts about yourself which will produce a healthy body, soul, and spirit. It's time to break free from the toxic thinking you have been feeding your mind. By reading and believing the truths below, you are nourishing yourself with the living Word.

> There is therefore now no condemnation to those who are in Christ Jesus.
> —Romans 8:1

> For I will forgive their iniquity, and their sin I will remember no more.
> —Jeremiah 31:34

> In this is love: not that we loved God, but that He loved us and sent His Son to be the propitiation (the atoning sacrifice) for our sins.
> —1 John 4:10, amp

> The Lord redeems the lives of His servants, and none of those who take refuge and trust in Him shall be condemned *or* held guilty.
> —Psalm 34:22, amp

> And, beloved, if our consciences (our hearts) do not accuse us [if they do not make us feel guilty and condemn us], we have confidence (complete assurance and boldness) before God.
> —1 John 3:21, amp

This is the process of getting free of guilt and the accusations of the enemy. After you get used to the idea that you are forgiven for your past, you will quickly recognize when it is the enemy coming to accuse you of your past.

2. When others accuse us

The second area of accusation is when others condemn us for our mistakes. This is often someone who may accuse us out of their own insecurities. Also understand that at times the enemy can *use* others to bring accusation against us.

Moving beyond our guilt and shame can be difficult when other people know our past. We can feel embarrassed by our actions, and we don't want to be defined by those past mistakes. When we know others are familiar with our past, we can sink further into guilt, shame, and condemnation.

Some people enjoy gossiping about our shortcomings because this makes them feel better about themselves. Insecure people have a need to put others down in order to puff themselves up. This is part of their problem and not yours. The Bible says that love covers a multitude of sins (1 Pet. 4:8). When someone cares about us, they don't gossip about our areas of struggle; they inspire us to overcome our weaknesses. Those people who truly love us and want us to succeed do not go around sharing our sins for their own gain.

When we feel the sting of accusation from others, it's important to go back to the Word and observe how God treated those who were repentant for their sin. We have already discussed at length two people in the Bible with whom God was very compassionate to. One is the woman caught in adultery, and the other is King David. In both of these examples, God shows His mercy and grace toward humanity. You and I are no different.

There is one more example from scripture that I would like to highlight. The scripture below shows two men who are praying to God. One man was a tax collector and recognized that he was a sinner. The Bible tells us he would not even look up to heaven but beat his breast and asked for God's mercy, for he was very aware that he was a sinner. This man had a repentant heart toward God. The second man told God how righteous he was, reminding Him that he fasted twice a week and paid his tithe, and thanking Him that he wasn't like other bad men, including the repentant tax collector. The irony was that Jesus favored the repentant tax collector. He said concerning these two men, the repentant tax collector will be justified rather than the other man. Read below the account:

> Two men went up to the temple to pray, one a Pharisee and the other a tax collector. The Pharisee stood and prayed thus with himself, "God, I thank You that I am not like other men—extortioners, unjust, adulterers, or even as this tax collector. I fast twice a week; I give tithes of all that I possess." And the tax collector, standing afar off, would not so much as raise his eyes to heaven, but beat his breast, saying, "God, be merciful to me a sinner!" I tell you, this man went down to his house justified rather than the other; for everyone who exalts himself will be humbled, and he who humbles himself will be exalted.
>
> —Luke 18:10–14

We see the heart of God in the above scripture; when we humble ourselves and repent to God, we are forgiven. Our guilt *can be lifted* when we choose to accept His forgiveness and recognize that our soul has been made clean.

Even if your accusers are speaking judgment against you, if you have repented and found forgiveness in the eyes of God, it doesn't matter what your accusers are saying. In fact, if they continue to accuse you after you have been made right in the eyes of God, they are stepping into the shoes of the high-minded Pharisee that we just read about. The man with the repentant heart was favored, forgiven, and released of his guilt more than the self-righteous man. Even if you are not able to address your accusers face-to-face, you can hold your head high and know that you are absolved from your past; you do not have to carry the weight of guilt and shame into your future.

3. When we accuse ourselves

There have been times when I experienced that sinking feeling when I knew I had done something wrong and I felt terrible about it. It's a nagging feeling of constant guilt. At times we mentally beat ourselves up for our mistakes, and it seems as though nothing can alleviate our sense of regret. In our mind we constantly remind ourselves of our mistake, saying such things as, "I can't believe I did that! How can I be so stupid?" Or, "I can't believe I said that! What was I thinking?" This type of dialogue plays over and over again in our mind, and extreme remorse sets in.

When this happens we feel ourselves spiraling down. It's at this point that some fall into a state of depression over their guilt. (We will be discussing more on depression in chapter 9.) We spend weeks, months, even years carrying around this guilt. Guilt says we are a bad person who has failed, and condemnation says we need to be punished for our sin. As we live under this weight, the mind and body also carry this burden; and that burden can spill out into emotional or physical sickness.

I would ask you, what is it that you still feel guilty over? Is there something that you did or said that you still feel guilt or regret for? And how do you rid yourself of these feelings? I am going to share a very powerful testimony to answer the question of how to rid yourself of strong feelings of remorse and guilt.

THE PLANNED VACATION

My husband and I and our two elementary school-aged girls, were getting ready to go on vacation. My husband and I had been telling the girls for weeks how great this vacation was going to be. We were headed south for the fourth of July to spend time with relatives. We were to stop in Virginia at Quantico military base to see my husband's son, who was in the marines at the time, and then on to Georgia to see my family. It would be a sixteen-hour drive that we were going to break up into two days.

A few weeks before the trip the enemy started to tell me all the horrible things that could happen to me and my family if we went on this family vacation. I was new to the principles of agreement, and I was new to spiritual warfare. I did not know that the enemy was sitting on my shoulder telling me tormenting thoughts.

When the morning of the trip arrived I was a nervous wreck. My husband had packed our SUV the night before so that in the morning all we had to do was get up and get in the car and begin our trip. I was shaking that morning as I got into the car because I was feeling like I could not make this trip. Everything in me wanted to scream, "I can't do this!" But, nonetheless, for my family's sake, I would go. We got on the highway.

For the next thirty minutes, I was having this battle in my mind: should I press through the two-day trip or should I go back home where I feel safe? After being on the road for about forty-five minutes, I turned to my husband and very sheepishly told him I did not think I could make this trip. He began to reason with me and encourage me that we would be fine. But it was too late. Nothing he could have said to me would have convinced me that I was going to be safe on this trip.

For weeks before the trip, the enemy had been tormenting me about this vacation; and I had yielded to Satan's lies. I had agreed with the enemy that this trip was not safe for me to go on and therefore I should not go. I did not go. My sweet husband turned the car around and we drove back home.

In this moment I felt smaller than a worm. I felt tremendous guilt and shame. I was telling myself I was the worst Christian, the worst wife, and certainly the worst mother. We got back home. At this point my husband, in his gentle anger, was upset. Could you blame him? He was looking so forward to this road trip. He called a family friend to come over and talk with me. My husband ended up going onto Virginia to see his son for a few days and then came back home.

During those few days I definitely felt the sting of self-accusation. I did the only thing I knew how to do, and that was fall on my knees in prayer. I spent time with God. I was continually telling God what an awful person I was and how I had no faith and didn't deserve to be called a real Christian. I figured that God was extremely disappointed in me for my lack of ability to trust Him to keep me safe on this vacation. (Have you ever been in a similar circumstance? If you have, read how God treated me.)

I remember one afternoon in particular, when I was telling God how awful of a person I was, that He interrupted me. As I had been praying that day, my eyes were shut; all of sudden it was though a movie was playing in my mind. I saw a beautiful ballroom, and I was in that ballroom in a beautiful ball gown. When I looked up, there was Jesus and He invited me to dance with Him. I immediately thought, "You want to dance with me? I don't deserve to be in such a beautiful place in this beautiful gown here with You; *and now You want to dance with me?*" Jesus smiled at me and held out His hand. Hesitantly I stepped forward and we danced. It was the kind of ballroom dance that was graceful and elegant, where the couple moved in perfect harmony. I followed His lead; and as we danced I could tell He was not angry with me, but quite the opposite—He was enjoying my company. I didn't want the dance to end. I felt safe, reassured, and beautiful in His presence. When the scene ended I opened my eyes with tears streaming down my face, and thought, "God, You're really not made at me or disappointed in me."

I understood in that moment that He saw beyond my mistake and right into my wounded heart. It was out of the wounded heart that I choose not to go on that vacation. God knew in the years to come that He would heal my bitter broken heart and my guilt. God restored me and I eventually went on several family road trips in peace. I knew in my heart that day that God was not angry toward me but instead He was full of grace, love, and mercy toward me.

Just as Jesus was with the woman caught in adultery and just as Jesus was with me, so God is with you. God knows we are imperfect people, and it grieves God when we don't accept His forgiveness. It's like a parent who sees his child suffering with affliction but the child won't accept *the way out* of his torment. Are you ready to give Jesus the guilt you've been carrying in exchange for His forgiveness of your past? There is a prayer below that you can say regarding guilt. You can come back to this prayer at any point in your life when you are facing times of guilt.

Prayer

Jesus, I come to You with this burden of guilt. I am tired and exhausted from the weight of guilt and shame. I no longer desire to walk with the embarrassment and shame from my mistakes. I ask You to give me the strength and the wisdom to trade my guilty past for Your great love for me. Holy Spirit, I ask You to show me if guilt and accusation tries to reenter my life. Help me to know that through Your death and resurrection, You nailed my sin, shame, and guilt to the cross. I accept Your redemption and I accept Your restoration in my life. I thank You that my past guilt no longer has a foothold in my life and I can be free to heal—body, soul, and spirit. I now understand that Your cross is enough to cover my mistakes. I thank You that You love me and desire for me to walk in physical, emotional, and spiritual health. In Jesus' name I pray. Amen.

Chapter 8

WORRY, ANXIETY, AND FEAR

*I*N THIS CHAPTER we will explore the topics of worry, anxiety, fear, and panic attacks. We will discuss some of the possible roots behind fear and how to heal from this toxic emotion. Worry, anxiety, and fear are tormenting and limiting. All three come from some level of fear.

I want to refer back to chapter 3 on the origins of negative thoughts. To refresh your memory, in chapter three we discussed three sources of negative thoughts. Any level of fear—worry, anxiety, panic attacks, phobias, etc.—can be traced back to those three sources of negative thought. Past traumas or abuses, generational patterns of thinking or generational curses, or demonically-inspired thoughts can all open the door to fear in our lives. Please keep this in mind as we go through this chapter on fear.

Fear attempts to stop us when we want to move forward. Fear tells us to sit down when we want to stand up. Fear controls our life to the point of putting limitations on us. Fear can make our life smaller and smaller, as with the case of phobias and panic attacks. Fear makes us feel worthless and like a failure.

I experienced years of panic attacks; and because of panic attacks, I felt devalued. What I didn't know during my time of severe panic attacks is that I was a wounded soul who was a work in progress. God was healing my heart and healing my thought life. The same is true for you if you're experiencing issues with fear—know that the Holy Spirit has a plan for your freedom.

HEALTHY FEAR VERSUS UNHEALTHY FEAR

We first need to examine the difference between unhealthy fear and healthy fear. This entire chapter is about healing the unhealthy fear in our lives, but there is such a thing as healthy fear. When God designed our brain, He wired our brain to send signals from the brain to the rest of the body to protect us.

For example, if you saw a bear in your backyard, there is a good chance that you would do something to protect yourself from the threat of the bear. Your brain would send signals to the rest of your body that there is a possible threat to your survival and you would do whatever it took to be safe. Another example is, if you were at a busy intersection you would probably *not walk* in the road for fear of getting run over by a car. Acute, short term, healthy fear can at times save our lives. I think most people understand and respect this concept.

What we're going to be discussing for the rest of this chapter is when we are faced with *irrational and unfounded* threats of fear. An example of this would be if you get a thought that you can't go to the grocery store today because you might pass out or some terrible accident could be awaiting you at the grocery store. After similar thoughts are repeated, you are afraid to go into a grocery store. This is the type of fear that is unhealthy and limiting. This type of fear attempts to steal your freedom and the very life that Jesus purchased for you on the cross. This is the type of fear we will be discussing.

The enemy uses fear

It needs to be understood that when there is a tragedy in our lives this can potentially open the door for the enemy to put negative thoughts in our life. I was vulnerable to the devil's lies of fear and what *could* happen to me because of the fear I experienced. I would get outlandish thoughts that would bring tremendous fear.

For example, I would get a thought that would go something like this, "If you eat this food you will get violently sick." This is in turn creates a fear or phobia from eating certain foods. If someone else got that same thought they would dismiss it because there was no basis of fear in them. They didn't experience the same kinds of trauma with fear, therefore they were not as susceptible to irrational fears and the lies if the enemy. I would get other fear producing thoughts such as, "When you're driving your car you're going to lose control of the wheel and crash into another car and get into a terrible accident." After months or even years of getting thoughts like that one, the last thing I wanted to do was drive for fear of what might happen. Some might say, "Those are irrational thoughts. Why don't you just get over it?" The simple answer is that I had little foundation for feeling safe in my life and a greater foundation of fear in my life; therefore, I was more open to tormenting fearful thoughts.

I used to feel very frustrated, even stupid at times, for falling prey to these irrational thoughts. I experienced a great deal of guilt and condemnation because I desperately wanted to be free of fear and worry but couldn't figure out how to get free. During this time of intense fear, my family and friends couldn't understand why I was so susceptible to fear. I used to get very down because I wanted to lead a normal life. But as I look back, I realize, though I struggled with panic attacks, dear friends of mine struggled with other things. Friends of mine had struggles with many other types of afflictions that I did not struggle with. I remember wishing my life was like other people, only to discover they too had their struggles. I used to think that if someone looked like they had it all together, they probably did. I was wrong. Even the most polished, educated, and talented among us have struggles. I finally understood we *are all a work in progress*. I now understand that no one leads a perfect life.

The enemy knows our vulnerabilities based on the hurts and traumas we've experienced. He uses what we've gone through to further beat us down. When those hurts get healed, the enemy has less control over our lives.

Once a traumatic event has occurred in your life, the brain will set off your alarm system in your body to prevent a similar trauma from happening again. Dr. Carolyn Leaf explains that when repeated negative thoughts continue in the brain, the brain develops structures of negative thoughts. The structures as she explains them are established in our brain but as we create new positive thoughts the negative structures are replaced.[1]

I've also learned that thoughts form neural pathways or grooves in your brain.[2] When we've experienced much fear, the brain can more easily go into that memory groove of fear. The good news is that this can be reversed.[3]

Some of us have had years or even decades of fear that now need to be replaced with scriptures that are the opposite of fear. This takes repetition and diligence. As I have said throughout this book, when toxic thoughts enter our mind, the mental stop sign should go up. This is where we say "stop" to that toxic thought of fear and we replace it with scripture. After we refuse to allow the negative thought to take up residency in our mind, we need to have a scripture ready to counteract that negative thought.

As I began studying and learning that previous exposure to real fear can open the door to irrational fear, I began praying and asking the Holy Spirit for help and a way out. It's very important that I, or anyone with a similar story, do not become a victim or use their past as a reason to stay stuck in any type of bondage. God's purpose is always to heal us so that we can then point others to healing.

Categories of fear

We are going to break fear down into two categories:

1. Anxiety or worry
2. Panic attacks and phobias

Understand that there are levels of fear. Fear can begin as stress, then move to anxiety and worry. If anxiety and worry are not diffused, then intense fears, panic attacks, and phobia's can develop. I will humbly attempt to reveal roots that keep us stuck in fearful thinking and how to begin the healing process from fear.

ANXIETY AND WORRY

The Greek word sometimes translated *worry* in the New Testament means to "take thought" or to be troubled with cares or to be *anxious*. So we learn that to be worried is to be anxious. Let's look deeper at this word. When I studied more deeply in the Greek, the origin of that word can mean to distract, to divide, and to separate into parts. What a word picture we get from the Greek! We learn that anxiety and worry are like fragmenting our mind into little parts. How are we to function successfully if our mind is fragmented and divided? I will be using the words *anxiety* and *worry* interchangeably.

Is God willing to help?

If we absolutely knew that God would help us, we would not worry or be anxious. So why is it that at times we struggle with believing that God will help us?

A friend of mine was going through a trial. In the midst of the trial he said, "I know that God *can* heal me, but *will* He heal me?" What my friend was saying is that he knew God had the ability and power to help; but would He help *him*? This echoes what the leper said to Jesus,

> When He had come down from the mountain, great multitudes followed Him. And behold, a leper came and worshiped Him, saying, "Lord, *if You are willing*, You can make me clean." Then Jesus put out His hand and touched him, saying, *"I am willing*; be cleansed." Immediately his leprosy was cleansed.
> —MATTHEW 8:1–3, EMPHASIS ADDED

I want to point your attention to the above italicized statements. The leper asked Jesus if He was *willing*. That word translated *willing* here in the Greek means to take delight in or to love. The leper was asking Jesus, "Do love me enough? Do you delight in me? Am I good enough for you to heal me?" Jesus responds back to the leper with the *exact same* Greek word of willing. Jesus said, "*I am willing*," meaning, "I delight in you; yes, I love you; yes, I will heal you." Isn't this the real issue? We fall into anxiety and all sorts of fears because we don't believe God loves us and delights in us enough to help us. You may think God comes through for others but not for you. This is illogical thinking.

If you feel God can move mountains for others but you're not sure He will move them for you, then it's time for a shift in your thinking. As you're thinking and worrying about your problems, begin to focus on the fact that God loves you enough to help you. Begin to shift your thinking to the truth that God delights to help you, He desires to help *you*. Remind yourself that He *will* work on your behalf. And then rest in His care.

Jesus' perspective on worry

Jesus talked about worry in the Gospel of Matthew chapter 6. In this passage Jesus admonishes us not to worry. He addresses four important areas in this passage: our value, our heavenly Father, our faith, and seeking God's kingdom first.

> Therefore I say to you, do not worry about your life, what you will eat or what you will drink; nor about your body, what you will put on. Is not life more than food and the body more than clothing? Look at the birds of the air, for they neither sow nor reap nor gather into barns; yet *your heavenly Father* feeds them. *Are you not of more value than they?* Which of you by worrying can add one cubit to his stature? So why do you worry about clothing? Consider the lilies of the field, how they grow: they neither toil nor spin; and yet I say to you that even Solomon in all his glory was not arrayed like one of these. Now if God so clothes the grass of the field, which today is, and tomorrow is thrown into the oven, will He not much more clothe you, *O you of little faith?* Therefore do not worry, saying, "What shall we eat?" or "What shall we drink?" or "What shall we wear?" For after all these things the Gentiles seek. For *your heavenly Father* knows that you need all these things. *But seek first the kingdom of God and His righteousness, and all these things shall be added to you.*
> —MATTHEW 6:25–33, EMPHASIS ADDED

I have italicized the four points that we need to get in our heart to remove or greatly decrease the amount of worry in our life.

First, Jesus points to the birds of the air and the flowers of the field and says, "Aren't you of more *value* than they are?" It's interesting that when Jesus speaks of worry He also speaks of our value. He makes the comparison between our value and the value of the birds and flowers. Why would He say that? He says that because some of us, like the leper from the previous scripture, don't feel valuable enough to receive God's help.

I still have to be careful I don't fall into this trap. Just recently some troubling circumstances came my way, and the first thing I thought was, "What if God won't help because I haven't yet perfected an area of my life?" It didn't take long before I realized that is a trap, and I quickly reminded myself of His wonderful care for me. We are never going to be perfect in all things and that should not hinder us from coming to God with our worries.

Jesus speaks to our worth and weighs our worth to the birds and flowers. Have you ever studied a beautiful flower in the spring? Have you experienced its vibrant color and the bright happy feeling you get when flowers grace the landscape? Jesus said that even Solomon in all his glory was not arrayed like one of these flowers. He says these flowers "neither toil nor spin" yet they are arrayed in beauty. God takes good care of the flowers; surely He will take care of you. How about the birds? When you hear birds chirping in the morning, it's likened to a reassuring song that says the day is going to be all right. Jesus says that the birds "neither sow nor reap" yet God makes sure they have food. Their needs are met, just like our needs will be met. The question for you to answer is, how much more valuable are you than a bird or a flower?

In times of anxiety when we are desperate, and in a state of worry, God is not going to check and see if we've been good or not before He intervenes on our behalf. When we have a relationship with God and our heart is turned toward Him, we can come to the Holy Spirit for help and God will come through for us. We are of more value than the flowers that beautify the landscape and the birds that sing their songs. You, my friend, are created in God's image. You are His thumbprint, His child.

The second interesting point in this passage is that twice Jesus refers to "your heavenly Father." A heavenly Father would be a protector, a nourisher, a father who looks after his child in a very loving paternal way. This is key! We will be vulnerable to worry and anxiety if we do not know that we have a loving heavenly Father who is capable and willing to meet our needs.

Perhaps some of you had a loving, reliable father and this concept is easy for you to grasp. But there are others who did not have a loving, reliable father, which makes this concept more difficult to grasp. We need to begin to look at God as a *loving Father* because that is who He really is. This is can be accomplished by renewing your mind to this truth. When you are facing a trial, you may have to repeat over and over, "God loves me, He is a good father, and He will work everything out for my good." We focus on this truth until it becomes a part of who we are. When worry attempts to overwhelm our thoughts, we need to remind ourselves that God is a loving father who knows how to take good care of us. When we keep our mind focused on who God is, we will suffer less from anxiety and worry and instead enter into emotional rest.

I remember years ago, when I started having anxiety attacks, I was in college in Connecticut and I was due to fly home to Missouri for the Christmas holiday. A few days before the trip, I started worrying about the details of the trip, including a layover that I would have alone. God showed me a scripture that became an anchor for me through and during that trip. The scripture was,

> You will keep him [or her] in perfect peace, Whose mind is stayed on You, Because he trusts in You.
>
> —Isaiah 26:3

The morning of the trip I said to God, "I'm going to see if your Word really works." (Keep in mind that I was very new in my faith; I normally don't test God. God was gracious to me.) This scripture says we receive not only peace, but perfect peace, *if* we keep our mind stayed on God because we trust Him.

During the trip thoughts of worry kept trying to enter my mind. I took that scripture and said it over and over again until I believed what it said. I kept my mind focused on God, and sure enough there was no fear. God did keep me in peace that day.

Jesus refers to God as our heavenly Father for a reason. A father is supposed to be the provider and protector for his family. God supersedes the definition of a good father because He is the ultimate provider and protector.

To provide means to supply someone with something, to make something available, and to support. *To protect* means to keep someone from being harmed or lost and to provide a guard or shield. Did any part of the definition jump out to you? If it did, I would write out the part that speaks to you and put it up in a place where you'll read it each day. This is part of renewing your mind to God's truths. When I read those definitions, it's like a soothing balm over my heart. I never get tired of His truth of love and protection.

When we read that God is our heavenly Father, our memory quickly looks for an example of a great father we may have known. As good as any earthly father could have been, they still pale in comparison to the "good Dad" that God is. As a good father will take care of their child and provide and protect, God will abundantly and in greater wisdom provide and protect us.

For someone who struggles with worry or any type of fear, this is a truth that is lacking. As I have continually sought God, I have found God time and time again to be an excellent Dad. I would do whatever it takes to care for my children, and God is a far better parent than I. Jesus said,

> For everyone who asks receives, and he who seeks finds, and to him who knocks it will be opened. If a son asks for bread from any father among you, will he give him a stone? Or if he asks for a fish, will he give him a serpent instead of a fish? Or if he asks for an egg, will he offer him a scorpion? If you then, being evil, know how to give good gifts to your children, how much more will your *heavenly Father* give the Holy Spirit to those who ask Him!
> — Luke 11:10–13, emphasis added

Again Jesus uses the term "heavenly Father" to convey the message that God will meet our needs. When we focus on the fact that God is our heavenly Father who knows how to protect and provide for us, we will walk in grater peace and less anxiety.

The third point Jesus address in this passage is our faith. When Jesus says, "O you of little faith," He is not mad at us; He wants us to trust in His care for us. It's as if Jesus is saying, "My beloved children, don't you know that I will meet your needs? Don't you know that I will care for you? Don't you know how much I love you? Have confidence that I will provide for you." The term translated *little faith* means lacking confidence or not having the assurance that God will come through. Jesus was giving us a tender rebuke for not trusting God. God is not angry with us when we fall into worry, but it grieves Him because He is able to help us in our weaknesses yet we won't trust him. God wants to help us, yet we don't believe He will come through for us. It is the same sentiment as when Jesus was addressing Jerusalem:

> O Jerusalem, Jerusalem, the one who kills the prophets and stones those who are sent to her! How often I wanted to gather your children together, as a hen gathers her chicks under her wings, but you were not willing!
> —Matthew 23:37

Again we see that God desired to cover the children of Israel under His wings, but they were not willingly. As we continue to get to know the protective heart of God, we can have the faith, the confidence, and the assurance that God will come through for us. Jesus' shoulders are big enough to carry our worries.

The fourth and last part of this passage that I wish to point out is also very important. Jesus says for us to seek the kingdom of God first and His righteousness and *all these things* will be added to us. When we seek God first, God will take care of our needs. If we focus more on our problems than God, we fall into anxiety and worry. When we run around in great distress and anxiety, we are putting our energy into our problems.

Recently my daughter was describing to me all the things she was worried about. She sounded very fragmented and very stressed. After letting her vent (because venting is healthy), I gave her some motherly advice and then encouraged her to turn her focus to her Helper, the Holy Spirit. I urged her to listen to the Holy Spirit's impressions and promptings concerning her problem. As she did this she was able to relax and eventually her problems worked themselves out.

There comes a fork in the road with our problems. When we have done all we know to do, we can choose to keep on worrying or we can say, "God, I've done my part. Now I am trusting You to do what I cannot." When we choose the latter path, we get to walk in peace. And if we choose peace, we will be healthier physically and emotionally.

To sum up Jesus' teaching in Matthew 6:25–33, we learn the four points He makes concerning worry. (1) We are valuable in the eyes of God; (2) we have a loving heavenly Father who desires to help us; (3) we need to put our confidence, our faith, in God's ability to care for us; and (4) when we seek God's kingdom first and His ways, He will intervene on our behalf.

Definitions

According to *Merriam-Webster, anxiety* is "a fear or nervousness about what might happen." And *worry* is, "to feel or show fear and concern because you think something bad could happen." The origin of the word *worry* is from "old English *wyrgan*; akin to Old High German *wurgen* to strangle." Sound familiar? Anyone ever felt strangled from worry? It's easy to see how the people in the middle ages got the word *worry*. They associated worry with the feeling of being strangled. Don't we do this to ourselves emotionally and even physically when we get wrapped up in worry?

So why do we worry? There are a few reasons that I have identified over the years that explain why we worry.

Worrying makes us feel safe.

Yes, I know it's hard to believe; but it's true. If we are worrying about a situation, we actually feel like we are doing something about the problem. When we worry we are like a gerbil on a wheel, going nowhere but feeling busy. Worry allows us a false sense of security that we are "working on it."

There are times when we face real problems, and there are situations that require us to take action. Instead of worrying we can get into problem solving mode. This is a healthy way to handle problems that come our way. Perhaps talking a problem through and looking at all the options for a solution will be helpful. Problem solving instead of worrying is a better way to handle situations. Getting counsel from people you trust can also be helpful. Bouncing ideas around with a trusted friend will also eliminate the need for worrying. Maybe taking out a sheet of paper and writing down all the positives and all the negatives concerning a big decision can be helpful.

But understand: to continue to stay in a state of worry will not solve a problem. Worry is a false sense of working on the problem.

Worry is a habit.

We have trained our brain to worry. Our mind goes on autopilot when it comes to worrying. Worrying comes natural for us because it's what we know, we are good at it. Chances are we have been practicing worry most of our life. We have trained our mind to worry.

We are so accustomed to worrying and trying to figure everything out that we run the risk of depleting our mental and physical energy. It may be time to break this habit. Research has shown that habits can be broken in twenty-one days.[4] Worry is a habit that, with the help of the Holy Spirit, we can change.

Worrying is passed down generationally.

I have already addressed the issue of generational patterns of thought, but it's worth noting in our discussion on worry that we definitely can learn the habit of worrying from our family line. If you suspect that part of your anxiety problem is generational, then I would encourage you to go back to chapter 3 and reread the section on generational thought. In that chapter there is the prayer to break generational curses. Go back to that prayer and say it with worry in mind.

Panic Attacks, Phobias, and Intense Fear

The Bible calls fear a spirit: "For God has not given us a spirit of fear, but of power and of love and of a sound mind" (2 Tim. 1:7). We become more vulnerable to a spirit of fear if we have past traumas, if we have ongoing mental stress, or if we have inherited the generational curse of fear. The enemy knows are weaknesses and our family lines and takes advantage of these. But don't be discouraged, because this spirit of fear can broken over a person's life. The cross of Jesus Christ is more powerful than any spirit of fear.

The famous evangelist Smith Wigglesworth tells the following story of an incident that happened with him and his wife, Polly:

> We were sleeping one night, when the manifestation of evil filled the room and the spirit of fear gripped both of us. Polly was so frightened she could not open her eyes. I suddenly sat up, in the bed, and saw the devil. I rubbed my eyes to be sure, it was him. I said, "Oh! It's only you." I then turned to Polly and told her to go back to sleep, it was nothing of consequence, and I laid my head back down. Suddenly an overwhelming sense of peace and love filled the room and we had the most blessed sleep ever.[5]

I have always admired this testimony because Smith Wigglesworth didn't give the devil any attention. As we get free from past trauma's and hurts and get free of generational curses, there will come a time when we too can say to the spirit of fear: "Oh! It's only you," and get back to living life. Put on you thinking cap and fasten your seat belt because here we go!

What is a panic attack?

A panic attack goes beyond worry, beyond anxiety, and beyond being nervous. A panic attack is an extreme state of fear. The panic state will begin as minor anxiety and then build to uncomfortable levels of anxiety; and if the fear is not diffused, the anxiety will escalate to a full-blown panic attack. I can tell you from my own experience that during the panic attack the mind and body go into the flight or fight response. This response prepares the body to either fight the threat or flee the threat. The threat can either be real or an anticipated threat that may never even happen. Many times just thinking about an event or situation can begin the cycle of anxiety and panic in the body.

There is an entire physiological response that the body goes into during a panic attack, fight or flight episode. This high level of panic usually lasts about ten minutes and then slowly the fear will dissipate. The body has worked itself up to fight or flight response (refer back to chapter 4 on stress). The fight or flight response releases a host of hormones including adrenaline and cortisol. These hormones are released to prepare the body for an emergency.[6] Once the panic subsides, the body has to get back to homeostasis, which is to get into balance and calm down.[7] After an episode of intense fear and panic, the body calms down, and fatigue usually follows due to the high levels of the stress hormones that were released.

In some cases the person's world may get smaller by saying to themselves, "What if I get a panic attacks while at the doctor's office or taking my child to the doctor or even going out in public places?" When a person begins to avoid going out in public places this is called agoraphobia.[8] I was agoraphobic, and there was a time when I would not leave my house. That was a very long time ago, and it took applying the principals in this book that set me free of agoraphobia.

I will be discussing a few possible roots that explain the "why" behind a panic attack someone experiences. Below you will find possible symptoms that someone may experience during a panic attack. I have created the following list of the physical and mental symptoms that I have experienced during panic attacks. These are confirmed by the many Websites that deal with this.

Physical and Mental Symptoms That Can Be Associated with a Panic Attack

- Heart rate increases
- Breathing becomes labored
- Feeling like you can't catch your breadth
- Sweating profusely
- Feelings of stomach aches, nausea, or diarrhea
- Begin to feel dizzy
- Arms or legs begin to shake

- Thoughts begin to race
- Feeling like you're in a tunnel
- A flood or rush of intense unexplainable fear
- Feelings that you're going to lose control, pass out, go crazy, or die

Having a panic attack can be a terrorizing experience. We were not designed to live in continual fear and terror. If you are someone who experiences panic attacks or you know someone that does, hang on because I hope to shed some light on why someone has panic attacks and how to heal from these tormenting episodes. We will be discussing three reasons, or roots, behind panic attacks. This list is not exhaustive; there may be other reasons why someone experiences panic attacks, but these are the most common I have researched and experienced. The first one is that panic attacks can be experienced because of a past traumatic experience. The second reason is because of a long phase of mental stress and pressure. The third potential reason why someone may experience a panic attack is that it could be generational.[9]

Past traumatic experience

The first reason a spirit of fear can attach itself to our lives is because of past traumas or abuses in our life. God created our brain to protect us. If a situation or an experience caused us to have tremendous fear, then in order to prevent us from having *another bad experience* our bodies may go into the flight or fight response (a panic attack) to keep us from the perceived danger. Remember, during a panic attack the flight or fight response kicks in so that we can either fight a threat or flee from a threat.

I have already shared that as a child I was exposed to very fearful circumstances. If my brain senses that I am about to be in a similar situation where I could potentially relive that same traumatic event, my brain would potentially start the early stages of a panic attack (the flight or fight response) in order to protect me from another fearful experience. The problem here is when there is no real threat to our well-being and yet we still go into a panic attack.

This can also be experienced from those who suffer with post-traumatic stress disorders. The enemy has attached itself to the person suffering with post-traumatic stress disorder and when that person's memory is triggered the brain starts the fight or flight response to protect that person from reliving another fearful experience. In essence, the memory is triggering the fear response. With this type of fear, we still go into the panic when there is no real threat because there is usually someone or something in our present situation that is *triggering* the fear response. The brain relates something that is currently going on to a fearful experience from the past.

Our goal, with the help of the Holy Spirit, is to uncover the unresolved roots that are buried in our soul that keep triggering the panic attacks. Understand also that the enemy of our soul feeds on those hidden heart wounds, and this makes it very easy for a spirit of fear to torment us.

Panic attacks and intense fear can make you think that you are either going to die, lose your mind, or end up in the hospital. Once someone has had a panic attack in a certain place or because of certain situation, that person can potentially begin to avoid that same place or same situation for fear of having another panic attack.

This can begin the cycle of avoidance behavior. It's in the avoidance behavior that "phobias" can develop. For example, if a person had a severe panic attack while at the dentist office, the person deems that the dentist office is no longer safe and now that person has a phobia of going to the dentist. The brain says I'm going to go into the flight or fight response to protect you from reliving a traumatic event.

The reason someone could go into a panic attack at a random place like the dentist is because *something reminds the person of a past trauma that they lived through* and all it will take is *a reminder of something associated with that past trauma* to kick off the flight or fight response (a panic attack) in the body. So when the person goes to the dentist and has a terrible panic attack and thinks the panic attack came on out of nowhere and doesn't know why that happened, the truth many times is something about the dentist office reminded the brain of a past trauma. In the example of the dentist, it could be a feeling of being trapped in the dentist chair, perhaps the person was trapped in an abuse. The dentist could make the person feel vulnerable at the hands of stranger and perhaps the person was traumatized by a stranger; this could kick off a panic attack.

Again, what triggers a panic attack is very individual; but something triggers the panic attacks. The person just sees the *surface issue* of: "I had a terrible panic attack at the dentist and now I'm never going back to the dentist," thus a phobia of going to the dentist develops. In this example the person may avoid the dentist for months, years, or even decades instead of dealing with the root issue behind the panic attacks and getting healed of whatever is really bothering them. I'm going to give you some ways to identify those hidden hurts in just a bit if you don't already know what hurts from the past are still bothering you.

As in the case of phobias, the spirit of fear knows that there is a hidden root behind the fear of an object or the situation. Phobias can be an illogical way for some to either protect themselves or punish themselves.

Season of intense stress

Another reason for a panic attack is if a person has had a long season of intense stress, worry, and ongoing problems. The mind can only take so much mental strain and pressure. If there is no emotional rest and peace, then panic attacks could occur.

The best illustration of this is of a teapot. If a teapot is put on heat and the heat continues to rise, eventually when the teapot hits it boiling point a whistle blows and steam comes out. We are like that teapot. We can only take so much heat before we reach our boiling point. The stress and pressure are going to come out in some way and a panic attack could be the result of ongoing mental pressures.

Keeping our peace and finding some joy in the midst of difficulties is imperative to our emotional and physical health. If the enemy knows we are under constant pressure with no relief, we are more susceptible to buying into his lies of fear. If you're finding that you're struggling with chronic stress, I would recommend that you go back to chapter 4 on stress and reread the chapter. We want to avoid excessive amounts of negativity and mental pressure in our life.

I remember hearing of a famous person who all of a sudden began to have panic attacks. Her doctor was wise enough to know that it was the excessive stress in her life. The doctor told her to get away, go on an extended vacation, and let her mind rest. She followed her doctor's advice, took a break, and changed her schedule around; and the panic attacks went away.

You may not be able to go on an extended vacation, but you can and must make some positive changes in your schedule.

Generational issues

The last root behind panic attacks that I will be discussing is *generational*. This was a cause behind worry and it's a cause behind panic attacks. Understand that worry is a milder form of fear; and when worry and anxiety get out of control, panic attacks could follow. Thus fear could also be part of a generational curse in someone's life. Perhaps a relative experienced panic attacks and now you find yourself suffering from them. It maybe that there was a severe trauma or abuse *in one of your ancestors* and they began having panic attacks, so now anxiety and panic attacks have become a learned thinking pattern running down your family line. If this is the case, then I would refer you back to chapter 3 to reread the discussion on generational curses and pray the prayer at the end of the chapter to break the generational curses in your family line.

The dominos

We read the scripture teaching us that there is a spirit of fear. One day I asked God during church: "Is the fear coming solely from my own mind or is the enemy trying to put fear on me?" Right away God showed me a picture in my mind of a row of dominos. What God showed me is that all the devil has to do is hit one of those dominos and then it's up to us whether or not we stop the rest of the dominos from falling. That's how our thoughts are, like dominos falling. The devil can whisper one fearful thought in our mind, and then we can choose to either dwell on that thought and get more and more fearful or replace the fearful thought with a truth from the Bible and stop the remainder of the dominos from falling. As I began to get healed of heart wounds and handling long-term stress and the generational curse of fear, I noticed I was able to stop the rows of dominos from falling a lot sooner.

In summation, what makes some people more susceptible to tormenting fear and panic attacks? Previous traumatic events, long periods of stress, and generational issues can result in panic attacks. There may be other reasons for panic attacks, but the previous reasons are the most common. When the person deals with the root causes behind any of the three reasons I have listed, the fear begins to fade.

THE OPPOSITE OF FEAR

Many people think that the only opposite fear has is faith. While it is true that fear and faith operate in the same way, there is more to this story. Faith is the belief that something good is about to happen before it actually occurs. Fear on the other hand, is the belief that something bad is about to happen before it actually occurs. Both fear and faith operate by the same principle—believing something before it happens.

The problem with telling someone, "If you had more faith in God's protection then you wouldn't be afraid," is that it brings condemnation. I had several well-meaning people tell me to simply have more faith and the fear would go. I felt condemned. I would get down on myself because I thought if only I could have enough faith then I wouldn't fear. This was incorrect. Yes, it's important to have faith; but if you're missing one key ingredient you will not get over fear. There is one common root that most fear sufferers share; that one root is the lack of genuine love in their life. That is not my opinion; that is scripture.

> There is no fear in love; but *perfect love casts out fear*, because fear involves torment. But he who fears has not been made perfect in love.
> —1 JOHN 4:18, EMPHASIS ADDED

One of the most important keys to becoming free from any type of fears is *love*. The meaning of the word from which *fear* is translated in this scripture is the Greek word *phobos*. This is the word from which we get our word *phobia*. This word means alarm or fright or exceeding terror. This scripture tells us we can cast this type of fear out through *love*—the God kind of love. The Greek word for love is *agape*. *Agape* love means to dearly love or to have affection for. This word also means God's chosen and God's beloved.

When a person doesn't experience the God kind of love, they don't have the perspective of how much they are loved and *protected*. The following statements hold much truth:

- Lack of love and the presence of Fear go hand in hand.
- Fear is directly tied to not feeling loved and not feeling safe.[10]

When someone who is stronger than you (God) and your earthly father loves you, you feel safe, protected, and secure; hence, there is no room for fear. The opposite is also true. When you don't feel loved by God (God always loves us but we don't always feel that love from God) and you didn't feel love from your father, then it's easier for fear to creep in your life. I have talked with many, many people regarding panic attacks, and there is usually a common thread among panic attack suffers: at some point in their life they did not feel loved and protected.

How I began to feel God's love is when I began to surround myself with scriptures and music that taught me how much God loves me. A couple of my favorite scriptures on this subject are God talking to us through His Word in the Song of Solomon. God says to us in the Song of Solomon:

> You have ravished my heart With one look of your eyes.
> —Song of Solomon 4:9

> Turn your eyes away from me, For they have overcome me.
> —Song of Solomon 6:5

When I first read those scriptures, I thought to myself, "God, do You feel that way about me?" And the answer was yes, He feels that way about you and me. Stop and think of it; the God who created everything says to you, "You delight My heart." The scripture says when you look at God, you "overcome" Him. This is saying God is absolutely crazy about you. When you get a revelation of this, fear begins to fade. The Song of Solomon brought such healing to my understanding of God's love that I wrote a book, a commentary on it. The Song of Solomon is known to be about the love between a husband and wife, but if you dig deeper it's actually a love letter from God to man, from Jesus to His bride.

I began to saturate my thinking with the depth of God's love for me, and this helped me to realize I was protected by Him. I began to hang scriptures on my refrigerator, my mirror, any place where I would see them each day. I began to believe that God really had my back and that He would care for me. God says to seek Him with all your heart and when you do this, you will find Him (Jer. 29:13). I was desperate to know Him, so I sought Him in Scripture and in worship. When we do this, He never fails to show Himself to those who are seeking Him.

Steps Toward Healing

I want to spend some time talking about the first root behind panic attacks—the root of past traumas, past abuses, and heartbreaks—because this can be the most common root behind intense fear. This is the most common reason for panic attacks and phobias. The question that can be asked is how do we heal from these wounds of hurt and trauma in our lives?

The first step is to *identify* what the hurt or trauma is. Sometimes our experiences are so painful that after we get through them we stuff them deep within our soul never to speak of them again. The subconscious mind stores our emotional pain. Someone may say something to us that triggers our emotional pain. We may see something that triggers the emotional pain from years ago. Whatever the trigger is, it is better to find healing for these hurts and traumas than be set off into a panic attack because of them. Our buried hurts will come out in some form if we don't deal with them. Our hurts and traumas can also come out as emotional or physical sickness. Remember, the CDC has said that 80 percent all illness has a "stressor" behind it.[11]

I want to pause and say that God can instantly heal us of past hurts and traumas. I've heard testimonies of God instantly healing people from horrible abuses that they suffered. The Bible tells us that God's ways are higher than our ways (Isa. 55:9). I want to encourage you to follow the leading of the Holy Spirit in how He wants to heal you. If you find that God does not instantly heal you, then walk out the process of seeing if your soul needs healing.

The first step in healing from our past traumas is to identify what the trauma or hurt was. You might say to yourself, "Well, *how* do I identify what the trauma or past hurt is?" If the tragedy or trauma you went through is not in the forefront of your mind, then ask the Holy Spirit what wounds are keeping you bound.

Let me explain. How serious are you about getting free from fear? If you are desperate then your healing is going to require seeking God. By this I mean it's going to require you putting yourself in a position to hear from God. For example, you should read your Bible every day. If you don't know where to start reading, start in the psalms or in the Gospels. By reading the Bible you are putting yourself in a position to let God speak to you through His Word. There were times that I would be reading the Bible and a scripture would jump off the page to me. When this happened I knew that God wanted to speak something to me to help me unravel the wounds in my soul.

Another way that I desperately sought God out was in my own personal prayer and worship time. We all need to find some time in our day to connect with God. There were times when I didn't know what to pray so I would pray the Lord's Prayer (Matt. 6:9–13), or I would plainly talk to God and tell Him I needed His wisdom and help. I would also put on worship music and ask the Holy Spirit to show me what past memories needed to be dealt with. The Holy Spirit is the best counselor and God does not want us to stay bound up in our pain.

Also, seeking God also means faithfully going to church: a church where the pastor is presenting a message from Scripture. God is waiting for us to pursue Him, to seek Him. Jesus said,

> Ask, and it will be given to you; seek, and you will find; knock, and it will be opened to you.
> —Matthew 7:7

This concept of seeking God is echoed in the Old Testament as well. In Jeremiah God says,

> And you will seek Me and find Me, when you search for Me with all your heart.
> —Jeremiah 29:13

This is one of the ways to get free from the past wounds and trauma. Yes, we can go to a counselor and talk through our problems; and I would say that can also be very helpful. But if you're going to a counselor for years and decades and you're still stuck in emotional pain from the past, then it's time to go on a mission to seek the counsel of the Holy Spirit. In fact, some prefer to do that first, or seek the Holy Spirit in conjunction with seeing a Christina counselor. The Holy Spirit knows what to reveal to us to be healed of that pain. Sometimes just confronting an emotional wound would set me free. When hurts are buried so deep in our soul it is almost a shock when that pain is exposed.

I believe the Holy Spirit is inviting someone right now to get on their knees and get serious about seeking God for what's keeping you bound. You may want to set the book down and pray and ask the Holy Spirit to give you wisdom in the days and weeks to come about what issues in your life need to be looked at and dealt with.

In addition to seeking God through reading the Bible, prayer, and attending church, we can also ask the Holy Spirit to help us identify hidden hurts in a few other ways. When I was feeling fearful, I would journal and write how I was feeling and hidden hurts would pour out of my soul. Other times I would discuss what I was going through with a good friend and hidden hurts would come to the surface.

I remember once I was talking to a good friend about my stepdad and in the course of the discussion I began to recall how my stepdad would have a gun and threaten us. I forgot that detail, and it was in talking that it came out after twenty years. When I was able to identify a certain wound in my life, I would walk around for a couple of days almost in shock that a particular detail lay dormant for so many years. I would say to myself, "I didn't even know that hurt was there." Understand that this is one of the ministries of the Holy Spirit, to reveal those hidden wounds of the heart.

After we identify those wounds then we need to *grieve over those areas of brokenness*. Most people skip this important step. This chapter is not adequate to discuss all the specific wounds that kept me bound to panic attacks, but perhaps I will one day write a book on that very subject. But for our discussion here, we need to bring our hurts and traumas out into light. Once we identify our hurts and wounds, then we *grieve over the pain* and in some cases the loss. Grieving over a past hurt would mean that I would cry over it, talk to a good friend about it, and pray to God about it *until the hurt, disappointment, and even shock of it faded*.

The next step is to *forgive those that need to be forgiven*. We will never be free of afflictions without first forgiving. By not forgiving someone we hurt ourselves not the other person. In the Matthew 18 Jesus tells a parable that gives the message that if we don't forgive, the tormentors are released in our life (see Matthew 18:32–34).

I have dedicated an entire chapter to unforgiveness (chapter 11). Many of us don't really understand what forgiveness is and is not. If you are unsure of how to forgive, it is my prayer that you will read the chapter on unforgiveness and gain new insight on the process of forgiving.

Once we have identified the pain, grieved over the hurt, forgiven those that wounded us, then we need to let it go in prayer.

Be patient in this process; because we don't get entangled with fear overnight, and it will take time to get untangled from fear. Rest assured, the Holy Spirit is the best to detangle. It takes time to change your way of thinking in regards to worry and panic attacks. For some of us, our brain is accustomed to thinking a certain way and it will take time to replace the lies of fear with the truth of scriptures. The Holy Spirit is the one who will lead you into all truth (John 16:13) to help you break this cycle of fearful thinking.

When I first began this process of understanding why I was such a worrier and why I was experiencing terrible panic attacks, I was desperate for answers. The truths that I have shared in this chapter were learned over a couple of decades. I would encourage you to work on one or two issues at a time as the Holy Spirit points to different heart wounds. God did not reveal all the emotional pain I was carrying all at once; it would have been too much for me to deal with. So don't be discouraged if your healing is a process.

There were many times I wanted a quick fix. I wanted to *do something* so that suddenly I would be instantly free; but that's not how it worked. There were layers of emotional healing that needed to occur. Each time God showed a hurt and I identified it, grieved over it and forgave either someone else or myself. Each time I did this, I could feel myself gaining freedom over fear. It eventually got to the point where areas where I used to fear no longer bothered me. We are all a work in progress. There are still a few more areas of my life I'm working on with the Holy Spirit, and I am confident He will lead me into continued levels of freedom.

I remember the first time my nineteen-year-old daughter took an airline flight by herself. She left out of one of the New York airports alone. We had made her reservations a couple months before her trip, and I wondered if I would be nervous for her the day of the trip. The morning of her flight I was fine; I had a peace that everything was going to be okay. There was only one point in which I had a wave of fear rush over me; that was the enemy trying to sit on my shoulder and bring fear. I told myself the truth in the situation, that she would be okay. That fear left. After her flights were over, I could see how fear did not get control over me. I want to encourage you that the day will come when you step back and see how far you've come in gaining levels of freedom from fear.

We are being led by the Holy Spirit to either prevent us from emotional bondages or dig us out of emotional bondage. If you struggle with worry, fear, or panic attacks, you may want to go back and reread this chapter. And each time you do, ask the Holy Spirit to show you something in your heart that needs to be healed. You would be amazed at what God will reveal to you when you ask Him.

For further help there is also the companion workbook to this book (available at www.luanndunnuck.com), which is geared to help you discover the roots behind your fear.

PRAYER

Below is a prayer to commit your fears to God and to reveal any roots or hindrances that have kept you bound to fear.

> *Holy Spirit, I ask You to reveal the known and unknown roots behind my fear. I am tired from this tormenting spirit of fear, and I look to You to show me the way out of fear. I understand that I have felt a lack of love in my life and I can now rest securely in Your love and protection. I confess my agreement with the spirit of fear, and I pray You would show me how to shut the door to the devil's foothold of fear in my life. I pray You would supernaturally reverse the negative effects that fear has had on my mind and my body. In faith, I thank You for showing me how to walk in godly peace. In Jesus' name I pray. Amen.*

Chapter 9

DEPRESSION

According to Merriam-Webster the basic definition of *depression* is "a state of feeling sad." It's where a person feels hopeless and unimportant. The opposite of depression is happiness, contentment, and delight. Is it possible to live a life free from long-term depression? Before I answer that question, understand that freedom from depression does not mean freedom from all discouragement, "rainy days," or seasons of being in a funk. Jesus said, "In the world you will have tribulation; but be of good cheer, I have overcome the world" (John 16:33). There will be times when life looks impossible, when circumstances seem overwhelming; but it's in these times that we can thrive if we get in God's presence, in the Word of God, and choose to be around godly people. The good news is the Bible says, "A righteous man may fall seven times And rise again" (Prov. 24:16). We may fall down, but as a Christian, with the leading of the Holy Spirit, we will get back up. To answer whether it is possible to live free from long-term depression, the answer is yes; it is possible to live free from a continual dark cloud over your life.

We are going to look at what science has to say concerning depression and also what the Bible has to say about depression. And don't worry; if you haven't already figured it out, I am not the kind of person that would say, "Just snap out of it." When people say things like this it can be bring a sting of condemnation. Thus far in the book, in each chapter, I have gone deeper to find the root causes behind the afflictions we face. Depression is no different.

WHAT SCIENCE HAS TAUGHT US

As I researched the medical side of depression, I found what many already know: people who suffer from depression may have a chemical imbalance in the brain, specifically lower serotonin levels in the brain.[1] I also found that the "the hippocampus, a small part of the brain that is vital to the storage of memories, appears to be smaller in some people with a history of depression."[2] The hippocampus is part of the limbic system, and the limbic system is the, "system structures that are involved in many of our emotions and motivations, particularly those that are related to survival."[3] Science also points to stress or major life crises that can bring about depression in a person's life.

The Mayo Clinic says the following about depression,

> It's not known exactly what causes depression. As with many mental disorders, a variety of factors may be involved, such as: **Biological differences.** People with depression appear to have physical changes in their brains. The significance of these changes is still uncertain, but may eventually help pinpoint causes. **Brain chemistry.** Neurotransmitters are naturally occurring brain chemicals that likely play a role in depression. When these chemicals are out of balance, it may be associated with depressive symptoms.(chemical imbalance) my words in italics. **Hormones.** Changes in the body's balance of hormones may be involved in causing or triggering depression. Hormone changes can result from thyroid problems, menopause or a number of other conditions. **Inherited traits.** Depression is more common in people whose biological (blood) relatives also have this condition. Researchers are trying to find genes that may be involved in causing depression [generational]. **Life events.** Traumatic events such as the death or loss of a loved one, financial problems, high stress, or childhood trauma can trigger depression in some people.[4]

The Mayo Clinic identifies five possible reasons for depression: (1) biological differences, changes in the brain; (2) brain chemistry, neurotransmitters which are brain chemicals; (3) hormonal changes, as in possible thyroid issues; (4) inherited traits from family, possible inherited genes that causes depression or generational issues coming down the family line; and (5) life events, as in major crises or stress.

The Harvard Health publication had this to say about the causes for depression,

> Research shows that the hippocampus is smaller in some depressed people. For example, in one MRI study published in The Journal of Neuroscience, investigators studied 24 women who had a history of depression. On average, the hippocampus was 9% to 13% smaller in depressed women compared with those who were not depressed. The more bouts of depression a woman had, the smaller the hippocampus. *Stress, which plays a role in depression, may be a key factor here, since experts believe stress can suppress the production of new neurons (nerve cells) in the hippocampus.*"[5] (Emphasis added.)

The women who had depression had a smaller hippocampus and the article cites "stress" as a suppressor of new cells in the hippocampus. Think of it, stress affects the production of new nerve cells in the brain, and to be healthy and less affected by depression we need the production of these nerve cells.

Both the Mayo Clinic and Harvard Health Publications cite issues that point to brain chemistry, hormones, and stress. Some may say, "I can take steps to reduce stress, but there is nothing I can do about a chemical imbalance in my brain or the hormones in my body"; but this is not altogether true. As I studied further, I found some interesting research about our brain chemistry and our hormones and how it relates to depression.

Below are excerpts from an article by psychologist Dr. Joseph M. Carver:

> Thoughts change brain chemistry: That sounds so simple but that's the way it is, with our thoughts changing neurotransmitters on a daily basis. If a man walks into a room with a gun, we think "threat," and the brain releases norepinephrine. We become tense, alert, develop sweaty palms, and our heart beats faster. If he then bites the barrel of the gun, telling us the gun is actually chocolate, the brain rapids changes its opinion and we relax and laugh—the jokes on us... What we think about a situation actually creates our mood... The brain is constantly, every second, pulling files for our reference. It scans and monitors our environment constantly. You've heard people compare the brain to a computer. Like a computer, the human brain has a huge database containing billions of files (memories) for our reference. As you read this document your brain pulls definitions of words or phrases. As we meet people during daily activities, the brain pulls their "file" for their name and related information.[6]
>
> When the brain operates on automatic, the files it pulls are greatly influenced by our mood. For example, if you are severely depressed, if your brain is left on "automatic," it will pull nothing but bad, trash, and garbage files... As long as the depressed brain operates on automatic, it will continue to make us miserable by pulling every file which has guilt, depression, and a bad mood in it. It will play a series of our "worst hits."... Remember, we can change files at will. Since the brain really doesn't care which file is active, a depressed mood can be changed by simply switching the brain to manual, taking more control over our thoughts.[7]

When we address the issue of a chemical imbalance, we learn from the above article (there are many articles by other professionals that espouse the same principal) our thoughts impact our brain chemistry for the better or the worse. In the first article it says our thoughts change our neurotransmitters on a daily basis. If you recall, the Mayo Clinic article cites neurotransmitters as being out of balance and this can be a contributor to depression. This is good news; *our thoughts impact the imbalance of neurotransmitters in our brain.* So when someone says, "I can do nothing regarding my brain chemistry"; based on the research, that is incorrect. As we change our thoughts, we change our brain chemistry. Let's keep going.

> [Dr. Carolyn Leaf] holds a Masters degree and PhD in Communication Pathology from the University of Pretoria, South Africa. Since 1981, Dr. Caroline Leaf has researched the human brain with particular emphasis on unlocking its vast, untapped potential. She has specifically focused on the cognitive neuroscientific aspects of TBI/CHI (Traumatic brain injury/Closed head Injury) and the science of thought as it relates to thinking, learning and renewing the mind, gifting and potential.[8]

Dr. Leaf teaches that,

> God designed the human brain in such a way that whatever you have wired in can be wired out. This is called neuro-plasticity...Humans are born with an optimism bias and it is our natural inclination to recognise and reach for the future. We naturally see the bright side of things. Negative thinking is a learned behavior...Negative thought patterns go *right down to our DNA and can be passed down to future generations.* These negative thought patterns lay dormant inside us until they are woken up, or we kill the thought! That explains how we see our children think like us and how we at times think the same as our parents.[9] (Emphasis added.)

She says the thoughts we have wired in can be wired out, and we have learned that brain chemistry can be changed by thoughts. This gives us much hope in dealing with depression because we are not at the mercy of our mood. Rather our emotion of sadness, our bad mood can be changed by changing what we are dwelling on.

Another source that draws the same conclusion is Dr. Lipton. He is a PhD, a stem cell biologist, a research scientist, and a former medical school professor. I have already cited Dr. Lipton in chapter one; but for our discussion on depression, this information is once again important.

> His experiments, and those of other leading-edge scientist, have examined in great detail the mechanisms by which cells receive and process information. The implications of this research radically change our

understanding of life. It shows that genes and DNA do not control our biology; that instead DNA is controlled by signals from outside the cell, *including the energetic messages emanating from our positive and negative thoughts*. Dr. Lipton's profoundly hopeful synthesis of the latest and best research in cell biology and quantum physics is being hailed as a major breakthrough showing that our bodies can be changed as we retrain our thinking.[10] (Emphasis added.)

And yet another source examines the relationship between our thought and beliefs and the healing of diseases.

Researcher Dawson Church, PhD, explains the relationship between thought and belief patterns and the expression of healing- or disease-related genes. Your body reads your mind, Church says. Science is discovering that while we may have a fixed set of genes in our chromosomes, which of those genes is active has a great deal to do with our subjective experiences, and how we process them. One recent study conducted at Ohio University demonstrates vividly the effect of mental stress on healing. Researchers gave married couples small suction blisters on their skin, after which they were instructed to discuss either a neutral topic or a topic of dispute for half an hour. Researchers then monitored the production of three wound-repair proteins in the subjects' bodies for the next several weeks, and found that the blisters healed 40 percent slower in those who'd had especially sarcastic, argumentative conversations than those who'd had neutral ones. Church explains how this works. The body sends a protein signal to activate the genes associated with wound healing, and those activated genes then code blank stem cells to create new skin cells to seal the wound. *But when the body's energy is being "sucked up" by the production of stress biochemicals like cortisol, adrenaline and norepinephrine*, like it is during a nasty fight, the signal to your wound-healing genes is significantly weaker, and the repair process slows way down. *By contrast, when the body is not preparing for a perceived threat, its energy stores remain readily available for healing missions.*[11] (Emphasis added.)

Let's look at one last area for another possible cause for depression—*our hormones.*

Hormones are molecules released by one part of the body to carry messages to another area in the body. The thyroid's main job is to produce just the right amount of thyroid hormone to tell your cells how fast they should burn energy and produce proteins. The adrenal glands' primary job is to produce just the right amount of stress hormones to help you to respond to all kinds and degrees of stressors... Think of the thyroid and adrenal glands as guardians, or protective intermediaries of the endocrine (hormone-producing) system. They both function as complex sensors, continually responding to ever-changing conditions within the body, and relay information back and forth between the brain and the body... The signaling for release of both sets of hormones originates in an area of the brain known as the hypothalamus, which sends hormonal messages to the tiny gland in the brain called the pituitary. From here, hormonal messages are relayed to both the thyroid and the adrenal glands. The adrenals and thyroid, in turn, produce hormones and provide feedback to the brain that says "that's enough for now!" We call these negative-feedback loops the HPA axis (hypothalamic-pituitary-adrenal axis) and the HPT axis (hypothalamic-pituitary-thyroid axis). A big adrenal response to a highly stressful event is normal. But afterwards, the adrenals need to rest. Much of the medical literature looking at the *effects of stress on the thyroid* has focused on hyperthyroidism and a condition called Graves' disease. In general, Graves' is caused by an autoimmune response that prompts the thyroid to make too much thyroid hormone. This is known to occur after a sudden stressful life change in people with a specific genetic makeup. But much less talked about is how *too much stress can also cause a slowing* of the thyroid, called hypothyroidism.[12] (Emphasis added.)

The cause of the hormone issues points to stress. Stress can cause the thyroid to make too much thyroid hormone, and stress can also slow down the thyroid function. Both can introduce physical problems. I researched similar articles as the one above and there is a great deal of information that says the same thing, stress (negative, toxic thought patterns) can affect our hormones.

Not only did I research this topic, but I have lived this topic. I know firsthand the dangers of allowing the enemy to plant seeds of negativity into our mind to the point that our thoughts become toxic to us. When our thoughts become toxic to us, our body is out of balance. Based on the above research, one could say our thoughts have created a "chemical imbalance" in our brain.

So what does all this research point to? Yes, there can be a chemical imbalance in our brain; and yes, there can be a hormonal response that may be triggering depression. The good news is that research is showing that as we change our thought patterns and beliefs, we will see a change in our brain chemistry and our hormonal imbalances. Research also points to our DNA changing based on the influence of our positive and negative thoughts. *To sum up the research, our thoughts affect our chemical and hormonal imbalances, which affect our levels of depression.* Science is catching up to the wisdom of the Bible telling us that as we think, so are we (Prov. 23:7) and to bring every thought captive to the obedience of Christ (2 Cor. 10:5).

The way we think is a habit, and habits take time to change. The above medical research is exciting because it shows us our brain is waiting for us to feed it good, godly, positive information. You might say, "I have no good, godly, positive information to feed my brain." Keep reading.

Depression from a Spiritual Perspective

If you or someone you love suffers from depression and they have been told they have a chemical imbalance, at the very least the question needs to be asked, "What is the person thinking about or dwelling on?" For the sake of our discussion on thoughts, let's look at the downward spiral of our thoughts.

- Negative roots (from hurts in our past or current crises) produce
- Negative thinking, which produces
- Toxic emotions, which produce
- Negative behaviors, which produce
- A poor quality of life.

Let's take our discussion on negative thought one step further. What is the source of our negative thinking? I answered this question in chapter three, "Origins of Negative Thoughts." I cited three sources or reasons why we fall into negative thinking: (1) past traumas and abuses, (2) generational issues, (3) and demonically-inspired thoughts. When someone is suffering from severe depression, they could be battling all three origins of their negative thoughts.

There have been times in my life when I have been under that dark cloud of sadness. I have had to step back and identify *why* I was feeling sad. Was there a past trauma that I was thinking on? Was there a current situation I saw no way out of? Did I find that other family members of mine also suffered from depression? Were my thoughts being influence by the demonic realm (i.e., the devil sitting on my shoulder whispering depressing thoughts to me)? These are questions that only the person suffering from depression can answer. As I have said throughout this book, you may want to answer these questions with a good friend or a Christian counselor, or perhaps you would prefer to journal. Ask the Holy Spirit to show you the source of your thoughts. He knows the exact roots behind your depression. Take steps to identify the source of your thoughts because the goal is change your brain chemistry by changing your thoughts.

Once I identify what's really bothering me, I will look to see if there's anything constructive I can do to change the situation. *If I can't do anything* about the circumstances, then I will look for the good in the situation. If I can't see any good in the situation, then I have to hand over my problem to God. In times when I can't do anything and I can't seem to find the good in the situation (which has happened many times), I surrender it to God in prayer. *I allow myself to grieve over what cannot be changed, and then I look to the future.* I look to God for the next steps for my life. If it's been a particularity difficult season of life, I will look for ways to revive my soul and get spiritually and emotionally refreshed. This could mean a weekend away, a retreat, or visiting with family and friends.

There are times when depression is caused by feelings of self-reproach and heavy guilt. If you suffer from not liking who you are or are feeling guilty and condemned, refer to chapter 6 on self-reproach and chapter 7 on guilt. Incorrect views that we believe about ourselves can also cause depression. Someone may see themselves as rejected, unlovable, a failure, and the list could go on.

In times when I held incorrect views of myself, I would find the opposite of these incorrect views, and I would begin to declare the *opposite* over my life. For example, if I was feeling rejected I would look up the opposite of rejected, which is to be accepted. I would then take the opposite and say something like, "I am accepted and there are many good things about me that are lovable." I would repeat this over and over for about two weeks until the old lie was pushed out of my brain and I established the correct view of myself. This was a process in my life of letting go of the depressing views of myself and replacing them with the truth. This is doing what Dr. Carolyn Leaf talked about, when she said, "What can be wired in can be wired out."[13] This is reversing those sad feelings and inadvertently changing our brain chemistry.

Below are a few scriptures that address the issue of sadness. These scriptures give us insight on how to counteract the sadness in our heart. I encourage you to really sit down, perhaps alone with a pen and paper or your spouse or with a trusted friend, and begin to answer the following questions concerning your life.

1. Proverbs 25:25: "As cold water is to a weary soul, so is good news from a far country." You need to have some good news back in your life. Begin to dream again.

- What would you want to wake up every morning and do if money was not an issue?
- What giftings and talents has God put in you?

- What is His purpose for your life? Really think about this.
- How can you to take small steps to seeing the above become a reality?

2. Proverbs 15:23: "A man has joy by the answer of his mouth."

- What areas of your life have you been speaking negatively about yourself?
- Have you spoken negative words over your future, over your family, over your health, over your finances, over your job?

When we speak negative over our lives we align ourselves with the devil. Take some time and repent to God for your words and ask the Holy Spirit to help you only speak good over your life, your family, your household, and your future.

3. Proverbs 13:12: "Hope deferred makes the heart sick." When you don't have hope, your heart is sick. "Heart" means your mind.

- What have you been waiting for that you haven't seen happen?
- Do your hopes, expectations or goals line up with God's Word?
- Do you feel you're in an Abraham or Joseph season where you need to wait on God's timing?

If you are in a waiting season, consider getting out and being a blessing to others. Sow seeds of encouragement, help, or even finances into someone else's life while you're waiting. I have spent a lot of time in this season and I know it is helpful to keep God's promises before you and ask God what areas of your life need to be cleaned up before He can bring those promises to pass.

JESUS' MISSION

The devil understands very well how we are wired—body, soul, and spirit—and he knows how to put sickness on us. He does this by tempting us to believe his negative, toxic lies. If we buy into the devil's lies and we dwell on his negative scenarios for our life, then we are headed for depression. Jesus came to fix the problem. Jesus is still doing the same thing for us today—fixing our problems. In fact, that was the reason Jesus came; He said so Himself:

> The Spirit of the LORD is upon Me, Because He has anointed Me To preach the gospel to the poor; He has sent Me to heal the brokenhearted,

> To proclaim liberty to the captives And recovery of sight to the blind,
> To set at liberty those who are oppressed.
>
> —Luke 4:18

In Closing

In closing this chapter on depression, I want to look at one woman's testimony of how she overcame her depression. I have reprinted her story of how she got free from depression:

> In a nutshell, I looked at all 3 areas of my life—body (exercise, eating habits), soul (thoughts, emotions, intellect, mind) and spirit (worship, faith, conscience, intuition). This is how I overcame depression:
> I started changing my eating habits and adding exercise to my routine.
> I changed the way I looked at myself and learned to love who God made me—imperfections and all.
> I started to blog and 'learned how to fly'!
> I started seeing myself as the new creation that I was and stopped seeing myself as I was before I was born again.
> I learned to replace the seeds of lies in my heart with God's truth.
> I started to worship God despite the black cloud that seemed to be my constant companion.
> I started to believe in a God who loved me just the way I am and understand His grace.[14]

Her story is inspiring and motivating. She looked at all three areas of her life—body, soul, and spirit—and observed where she could make changes. If you suffer from depression or times of discouragement, I would encourage you to consider putting into practice some of the principles found in this chapter of retraining and replacing your thought life. At the same time, consult and work with your doctor for your personal plan to overcome depression.

Prayer for Depression

God, I come to You tired of this battle with depression. Please give me the wisdom to know when my thoughts are producing the emotional and physical response of despair. I break all ties, alignments, and agreements that I have made with negative thinking concerning my life, my future, and my family. Holy Spirit, grant me the grace to see the good that You have in store for my life. I ask You, God, to bring times of refreshing and restoration to my life. In Jesus' name I pray. Amen.

Chapter 10

Anger and Bitterness

Anger can be likened to a tsunami in our soul. There is a rush of anger that floods through our veins when someone has hurt us, used us, or misunderstood us. When anger fills our soul, we feel like we are going to erupt if there is no resolution. If anger is prolonged with no outlet, then bitterness can set in. If the anger and bitterness are not resolved, then both will take root and yield devastation in us and our relationships.

The sly thing about these destructive emotions is that some of us don't even know we are angry and bitter. I have seen people completely in denial of these emotions. Anger can be very covert and will come out in other harmful ways. If anger and bitterness are not resolved in a healthy way, they can damage our emotional and physical health.

How can one escape the peril of both anger and bitterness? How can we stop the toxic effect of anger and bitterness in our life? I will be sharing nuggets of wisdom that the Holy Spirit has given me to escape the grip of both anger and bitterness. We will first discus the toxic emotion of anger.

Anger

Anger can be viewed from several different perspectives. The view that we will be discussing anger from is when someone has hurt us, betrayed us, or placed irrational demands on us and this causes an anger response in us. *Anger* in the Greek means violent passion or indignation; to anger someone means to provoke them to anger. We learn that certain things provoke us and bring forth these emotions, but learning how to handle our response and heal from our anger becomes imperative to our health. This is where people get stuck in this damaging emotion, and this is the perspective of anger that I will be addressing.

When anger arises in our life, it becomes like a ping-pong game. Someone hurts us with their words or actions, and we fight back with our words or actions; then they retaliate with their words or actions, and back and forth we go with no resolution. When we play this game, we are left not only angry and hurt but sometimes even sick.

Before we discuss toxic anger, I would like to clarify the difference between *toxic anger* and *righteous anger*.

Righteous anger

Righteous anger can be beneficial. Righteous anger can rescue, liberate, and restore people and situations. Let me explain. Righteous anger can cause people to seek justice where there's injustice. This type of anger motives us to correct inequalities and abuses.

An example of this would be if someone knows a child is being abused and they become angry at the situation. Because of their anger they will do something to rescue that child out of the abuse. This is righteous anger. Another example of righteous anger would be where one nation sees a smaller nation being overtaken by a dictator. The stronger nation steps in and defends the smaller nation from being overrun. This is righteous anger. Throughout history there have been numerous times where one people group has been taken advantage of by another people group. When this has occurred we have seen the righteous anger of individuals step in and defend the less advantaged group. This is righteous anger.

We even learn how Jesus' righteous anger brought about change. Jesus turned over the tables of the money changers in the temple. He told those who were buying and selling in the temple, that His house shall be a house of prayer (Mark 11:15–17). Jesus observed wrong actions in His church, and He dealt with those wrong actions to restore holiness back to God's house. This is righteous anger.

Righteous anger results in beneficial change, unlike toxic anger which creates turmoil in our life. Toxic anger results in the loss of our peace and in some cases our health. In righteous anger the unethical or immoral is recognized and there is a plan to liberate; whereas in toxic anger we become bitter and cynical. In righteous anger the end result is positive; unlike personal toxic anger, which can go on for years or even decades if not dealt with.

Toxic anger

Toxic anger comes from anger that is unresolved in our life. There are circumstances and situations that left us broken and frustrated and angry. Below is a list of a few reasons why we can be provoked to anger. There are other reasons for anger that are not listed below. If this is the case, write in your own origins of anger. The goal is to identify your anger.

- Anger that is the result from someone breaking your heart: This would be someone who promised you something and didn't come through for you. Or, it could be from someone in your childhood who was supposed to provide for your basic needs but did not.

- Anger at someone who has a "my way or the high way" mentality: They refuse to consider any other perspective but their own.
- Anger over someone who is irrational or illogical in their dealings with you.
- Hidden anger with someone who takes advantage of you, who continually uses you to get their needs met at your expense.
- Anger with a person who walks in pity (a "poor me" attitude or "no one has it as bad as me" mentality) and manipulates those around them.

Can you identify with any of these statements on anger? If you do, then there is a good chance that you have anger in your heart. The Bible gives us a few principles on how we should handle our anger.

The first one is;

"Be angry, and do not sin": do not let the sun go down on your wrath.
—Ephesians 4:26

God puts a time limit on our anger. Of course there are going to be times in our life when we get angry, but the key is to not to *stay* angry. Noticed the scripture says, "Be angry" but don't sin. Someone or situations may push your buttons and you're going to get upset, but the second half of that verse says "do not sin." This means don't retaliate or do anything foolish that may cause further harm. This verse is also teaching us not to keep anger in your heart for long periods of time.

If you don't resolve the anger than a root of bitterness will spring up; and if you allow a root of bitterness in, then unforgiveness sets in. And this is *destructive to you*! You might say, "Well, what am I supposed to do when I become angry?" There are two ways to handle anger.

1. Confront the issue in a gentle way.
2. Let it go and give the person or situation over to God.

To confront the issue in a gentle way means to go to the person and try and resolve the conflict. The Bible says, "A soft answer turns away wrath" (Prov. 15:1), and "If it is possible, as much as depends on you, live peaceably with all men" (Rom. 12:18). Anger can be resolved when both parties allow each other to share their perspectives. If this is not possible, then go to the second way to handle anger.

The second way to handle anger is to let it go and give the person or situation over to God. *Before you throw your hands up and say you can't do that*, wait; this is where the Holy Spirit gave me pearls of wisdom to learn how to let go of unresolved anger.

Ideally the best way to handle your anger is to be able to go to the person and share your heart with them (Matt. 18:15–17). It's best to wait until both parties have had time to cool off. In this process it's important to listen to the other person's perspective. Both parties should have an opportunity to share their hurts and disappointments. Most of the time, when both people have an opportunity to share their perspectives *and the other person listens* to the "why" behind their actions, reconciliation can be reached. In some cases both parties may want to have a "neutral" person or mediator present to help settle the disagreement. There may have to be some apologies made and perhaps a few tears shed, but reconciliation is possible.

I remember one experience where I was very angry because I felt I was put on the back burner by someone. I was very angry at first and then hurt set in. I felt hurt and rejected by the person. The anger eventually fizzled but I was still hurt. This is a key: many times *behind our anger is hurt and grief.* Jesus made mention of anger and grief in the Gospel of Mark:

> And when He had looked around at them with anger, being *grieved* by the hardness of their hearts, He said to the man, "Stretch out your hand." And he stretched it out, and his hand was restored as whole as the other.
> —Mark 3:5, emphasis added

Notice how Jesus expressed that He was angry *and grieved* by the hardness of their heart. The word translated *grieved* in the Greek means to be sorrowful. To be grieved means to be saddened. These two emotions often times go together. Grief follows anger as a result of someone wounding us.

Just like this scripture, the person who I felt put me on the back burner evoked anger in me which then led to hurt and grief. After I cooled down, I went and spoke to this person. It turned out there was a miscommunication between me and the person. I shared my perspective and they shared their perspective. We were able to respect each other's viewpoints and we were able to reconcile. In this instance getting together with the person and talking things out resolved the issue. This is a healthy way to handle conflict and resolve anger.

However, you can probably think of people in your life where sitting down and having a civil conversation with the person is out of the question. Perhaps the person is not willingly to sit down with you, or perhaps the person is deceased. This is where the *letting go and turning it over to God* has to be the way the anger is resolved so that *you can be free.*

An example of this is when I was in a relationship with a person who would not speak to me for periods of time because I was not able to meet their unrealistic needs. They were placing demands on me that were too much for me to keep up with. Every time I would see the person, I would get boiling mad because *I was trying* to be a good person and help them out but they continued to want more from me then I could give. They demanded too much; and when I couldn't meet their expectations, they would give me the cold shoulder and become angry with me. One Sunday in church I started thinking about all the times I helped this person but it was never enough. I became so angry over this situation that I started to go into a panic attack. I had not had a panic attack in almost a decade, and here I was in church so angry that my stress hormones started to kick in.

I was reminded that anger, like fear, can spin us out of control to the point where we go into the *fight* (anger) or *flight* (fear) response. In our body the same chemicals released in a panic attack are also released in an episode of anger. The body's stress hormones begin to kick in when anger floods your mind. You can feel your body chemistry change when you are confronted with fear or anger.

When this happened to me that day in church, I knew it was time to confront this person in a nice way and explain to them they could no longer lean on me the way they had been. As I attempted to share how I was feeling with the person, about two minutes into the conversation they blew up at me. I realized then that this person was not capable or willingly to sit down and have a civil conversation with me. I finally walked away knowing there was no way I could sit down and rationally talk with the this person.

So here I was stewing in my anger. For the next several days, every time I thought about the situation I would become even more upset. My anger toward this person was interfering with my daily life. Something had to change. I began to pray and ask the Holy Spirit to give me wisdom as to how to handle my unresolved anger. The Holy Spirit showed me powerful insights on how to let go of this anger. This was a pivotal time; because I could have decided to stay angry for weeks, months, or even years or I could apply these following principles to help me let go of the anger I had in my heart.

Below I have listed a few pearls of wisdom that helped me let go of this anger. I believe this same wisdom will help set you free as you apply these principles. As I stated earlier, with anger we either need to confront the person in a nice way and talk things out or let it go and give it over to God. What the Holy Spirit showed me helped to loosen the grip of anger over my life.

1. Reverse the anger.

After we have had a "blow up" or disagreement with a person, it can consume our days and nights. I remember losing sleep because of anger. For the first few days after the argument I replayed over and over the details of the argument. I thought about what I should have said and how I could have reacted. The more I thought about it, the angrier I became. I knew something had to change because I knew this anger was toxic.

This is the insight the Holy Spirit gave me: every time I would get anger thoughts toward that person, I would instead pray for God's blessing on their life. What the Holy Spirit showed me was that every time angry thoughts entered my mind about the person, I needed to say, "No, I'm not going to replay the anger in my mind. *Instead* I'm going to lift this person who hurt me up in prayer. I'm going to reverse this curse of being plagued by replaying the argument over in my mind and instead cover that person in prayer."

This became my MO (mode of operation). I would get an angry thought about the person or a situation, and I would pray blessings on the person or blessings over the circumstances. You understand this is spiritual warfare. When the devil tempts us with anger, we can instead pray for the person. The devil doesn't want us covering the person in prayer twenty times a day; he wants us stewing over the argument twenty times a day. Reverse the anger: instead of stewing in your anger, pray for that person. By doing this the devil will learn to stop tempting you to be angry because his temptations will result in a prayer covering for the other person. This is powerful.

2. Consider the source.

The Holy Spirit also showed me that the devil was using that person to get me sick in mind and body. The devil was sitting on my shoulder reminding me of what the other person did and how I should be hurt and angry. In essence he was using them to push my buttons. The devil many times is the source. He was sitting back laughing at me because I was buying into the anger and hurt he was feeding me.

I had to learn to separate the person from their actions. Sometimes the person needs help; if they were in their right mind they probably would not have done or said what they did. It's been said that hurt people will also hurt people; this is the truth. This insight caused me to change my perspective. Once I recognized the source of the anger was using someone else to get to me, I was able to separate the enemy from the person and have compassion on the person. I realized the devil was trying to put emotional and physical sickness on me by getting me riled up in anger. Once this truth became apparent to me and I understood the source, I was able to forgive that person and *give them over to God and let God bring healing to the situation.*

3. Repent for the anger.

When we spend weeks, months, or even years in anger, we have come into agreement with the devil. Remember, God commands us, "Do not let the sun go down on your wrath." This means not to stay angry for a long period of time.

We need to repent for doing the opposite of this scripture, which some of us have done by ignoring His command and staying angry. I recognized that I had done this and therefore needed to ask for forgiveness.

When we are in anger for long periods of time, we are taking God's place by not letting go of our anger until justice has been served on the person. We need to let God be the judge over that person's life. Our job is to forgive the person; God's job is to judge them. The same mercy we want extended to us in our wrong-doings, is the same mercy we need to extend to other people. Repenting from our anger and coming out of alignment with the devil is essential for letting go of our anger. God says to us, "Let all bitterness, wrath, anger, clamor, and evil speaking be put away from you, with all malice" (Eph. 4:31). We need to get in agreement with what God says.

I have had to apply the above principles to very difficult times of anger in my life. I will tell you that it takes time to change our mindsets about anger. If we have always stewed in our anger, it will take a conscious effort to replace our old ways of handling anger with new healthier ways. It *is possible* to not let the toxic emotion of anger control your life.

Very Important Lessons

We have been discussing how to handle anger when someone has *provoked us*; but what about when *we are the one doing the provoking* to others? Interesting thought isn't it. There is a possibility that at some point in our life we have said or done something that caused someone else anger, grief, and hurt.

What I'm about to tell you can help prevent conflict in your life and in the lives of others. We need to be very careful that we don't place unrealistic expectations on others. People will not always meet our expectations. When we get *demanding* of others, we very well may be provoking them to anger. Have you ever had a friend or relative who only sees their own perspective—only concerned with their own needs and time schedule? We don't want to be that person who is difficult to get along with. We don't want to be the type of person that provokes others to anger. This is wrong, and we need to guard ourselves from giving others a reason to become angry.

To address the issue of placing unrealistic expectations on others, it's important to step back and examine what we are asking someone to do for us. If what we are asking is beyond what the person is capable of doing, then we should reconsider asking. If we are stressing the other person out, then we shouldn't be asking. The bottom line is that we don't want to put our expectations on others and thus provoke them to anger. We don't want to unnecessarily *create* conflicts in our relationships.

This is can be common in families because family members can feel they have the right to impose without considering the capabilities or schedule of the other person. For an atmosphere of peace, it is essential that we are *thoughtful* of other people, especially family members. Let's be mature about our expectations of others.

When we put our needs high above others and don't consider the perspective of others, this is a cause for tension in a relationship. We want to avoid anger not instigate it. We can easily provoke others to anger when we don't look at a situation from the other person's perspective. Trying to get others to do what we want them to do is controlling. We probably would not do this intentionally, so it's helpful to ask the Holy Spirit to make us aware if we are being selfish. It's important to lay our will down and seek the will of God.

Whether we are the ones being provoked to anger or we are the one doing the provoking, we need to change our thoughts and mindsets concerning anger. For the sake of our emotional and physical health, let's be wise in our relationships with others.

BITTERNESS

I've heard it said that bitterness is a frozen form of anger, and it's true. When we choose *not* to let go of our anger, bitterness sets in and takes root. We have already discussed how anger can be toxic to us, but bitterness cements that toxic anger to our lives. When someone is bitter they are refusing to let go of the offense that was brought against them. We can be bitter over many things, such as loss of a job or income, a sickness, a relationship issue, or life didn't turn out as we had planned.

What keeps bitterness in place is when we replay the offense over and over again in our mind. We rehearse conversations, accusations, and hurts until we feel justified in our bitterness. The more we think about the circumstances, the more we want retribution. We think our bitterness is getting back at the situation or the other person, but bitterness is only harming us. Bitterness brings with it negativity, resentment, cynicism, and unforgiveness. We get stuck in bitterness and we miss out on what God has planned for our lives.

Bitterness is also harmful to our physical bodies. Below is a description of the effects of bitterness on the body.

Bitterness and the body

Pastor Henry Wright tells us not to take another person's sin into our body.[1] There is a lot we can learn from that statement. This refers to when *we allow* other people's actions to upset us to the point of becoming sick. Going back to one of the keys to becoming free of anger, remember we need to know the source. The enemy of our soul uses other people to "push our buttons" and then tempts us to remain in anger and bitterness. If the devil can get us to drink the cup of bitterness, then we have just taken some else's sin into our body. Below are a few ways that bitterness can steal our health:

> Feeling bitter interferes with the body's hormonal and immune systems, according to Carsten Wrosch, an associate professor of psychology at Concordia University in Montreal...Studies have shown that bitter, angry people have higher blood pressure and heart rate, and are more likely to die of heart disease and other illnesses.[2]
>
> "When harbored for a long time," says Professor Wrosch, "bitterness may forecast patterns of biological dysregulation (a physiological impairment that can affect metabolism, immune response or organ function) and physical disease."[3]

Bitterness is not worth you and me getting sick. Hormones, immune systems, organ functions, and the heart can be affected by carrying bitterness. As much as we have been hurt by circumstances or people, if we hang onto bitterness, the potential is present for us to get sick. The thought of developing an illness because of someone else's wrong behaviors is enough to make me drop the bitterness. "Your body responds to the way you think, feel and act. This is often called the 'mind/body connection.'"[4]

Whether it's bitterness or any other negative emotion, our bodies are listening to what's going on in our minds. This is too high of a price to pay for hanging onto bitterness. Remembering that we don't want to take other people's sin into our body, we should be motivated to check our hearts and discern if we are carrying any bitterness.

The Bible is very clear on the harmful emotional effects of bitterness. A bitter person believes their bitterness is justified, but the truth according to scripture is that bitterness contaminates our relationships.

> Looking carefully lest anyone fall short of the grace of God; lest any root of bitterness springing up cause trouble, and by this many become defiled.
> —Hebrews 12:15

Bitterness is described as a root. We know that roots are under the surface and cannot always be seen. We also know that roots produce a certain type of plant. In this case the plant represents our life and the root is the anger and bitterness that is lodged in our soul. If we don't remove that root of bitterness, that plant has the potential to be toxic in our life because the root is toxic.

Bitterness in this context comes from the Greek root meaning cut or prick. *Bitterness* comes from the Old English word meaning to bite. These definitions create a word picture for us of what bitterness can do in our lives and the lives of others. A root of bitterness can bite and pierce, and in this context it is talking about *us*, not the situation or other person.

This scripture goes onto say that this root causes "trouble." *Trouble* is translated from a Greek word that means disturb or cause a tumult. This scripture teaches us that the *trouble* bitterness can cause is to open the door to the demonic. If that revelation is not enough to make us run from bitterness, the scripture also says that many will be "defiled" by this root of bitterness. *Defile* means to pollute, contaminate, or corrupt. Have you ever been around a bitter person? Bitter people tend to change the atmosphere of a room and change the tone of a conversation. If you talk to a bitter person long enough, you can observe the anger and bitterness that resides in that person's life. The bitter person will try and get you on "their side." There have been times in my life and when I have done this. I have felt so hurt, angry, and bitter that I wanted everyone to see how wrong the person was toward me. This is wrong. I had to repent to God and turn the person and circumstances over to Him, because God knows best how to handle the situation.

The above scripture goes onto say, "By this many become defiled." As I mentioned, *defile* means to pollute and to contaminate. Bitter people have the potential to contaminate and pollute other people. They may gossip about the person or situation and may even plot against the object of their anger. This only leads to further destruction for them.

I have a family member who has been angry and bitter over a situation for three decades—thirty years is a long time. All I have to do is mention the situation, and the family member's countenance changes. Despite the amount of time that has passed, this person is still as angry today as they were so many years ago. The anger and bitterness is not affecting the person who hurt them three decades ago, rather the anger and bitterness is affecting this person today.

The questions arise: How do I know if I have bitterness? And, how can I become free from this toxic emotion? If you agree with any of the statements below about bitterness, there is a good chance you need healing in this area.

You know you have bitterness if you would agree with the following statements:

1. You know you have bitterness if *you want to see the other person get what's coming to them*. You declare, "What they've sown there

going to reap. You look forward to the day someone treats them the way they've treated you.

2. You know you have bitterness if *when you see the person out socially, you would not say hello.* I'm not advocating making the person your close friend, but we should at least be able to say hello (if the other person is willing).

3. You know you have bitterness if *you don't want to see the person receive God's favor and blessings in their life.* The person that hurt you could have offended you out of their own pain. God sees the deep things of a person's heart and He knows how to heal the person that hurt you; and that probably includes showing that person His grace and mercy.

4. You know you have bitterness if *you always speak negatively of a person or an event in your life.* When we continually "have nothing good to say" about someone or a past circumstance, then we may be carrying bitterness and resentment in our hearts.

5. You know you have bitterness if *you refuse pray for the other person.* Instead of praying for that person, you would rather tell God how that person or situation hurt you.

6. You know you have bitterness if *you wish your life would have turned out differently.* You are bitter over your current life circumstances. You may blame yourself, others, and even God. You have little hope for a bright future or anything good to come your way.

If you agreed with any one of the previous statements, then you are probably carrying bitterness. Bitterness can be directed against someone or a set of circumstances that have occurred in your life. The person or hurtful circumstance becomes a stumbling block for you. It's as though the bitterness prevents you from living in peace and from living out your God-given potential. We can also become embittered against God, which I will be addressing; but for now I have listed below practical steps we can take to heal and prevent bitterness from becoming a stronghold in our life.

1. Vent.

Allow yourself the opportunity to express how you have been hurt or wounded. This can be accomplished by talking to a trusted friend or a Christian counselor about the circumstances or venting through pen and paper. Sometimes the best way to get hurtful emotions out of your soul is to write them out.

When we vent by talking or writing, hidden hurts can surface that need to be brought to the light. When hurts come out of the dark, they are exposed and no longer have power over us. Venting allows us to get that toxic bitterness out of our soul.

2. If possible talk to the person.

Just like anger, the healthy way to dispel anger *and bitterness* is to go to the person and have a heart-to-heart talk. If this is not possible, then move right to number three.

3. Pour your heart out to God.

We can go to God in prayer and talk to Him like we would a best friend. We can even cry in His presence. Remember that tears are healing. Psalm 56:8 tells us that He puts our tears in His bottle. God is extremely compassionate towards us as we work through our pain. We can ask for His wisdom and grace in the matter.

If we turn to God, He can turn the hurtful events in our life around for good (Rom. 8:28; Gen. 50:20). Our pain can teach us about ourselves and how to treat other people. Seek God on how you can grow and learn from this experience. Repent to God for carrying such bitterness. Repentance of soul equals revival of soul.

4. Forgive the person.

As difficult as this may be, we still need to forgive the person and hand them over to God. The next chapter deals with how to forgive. Forgiveness is needed, especially when we think the person does not deserve forgiveness.

5. Look for the new beginning and the fresh start.

This is my favorite one. If we have experienced a bitter season of our life, hang on—things will improve with the leading of the Holy Spirit. There's comes a point where we need to let it go and move on.

A side note: if you are bitter over the death of a loved one, moving on from the place of your pain does not mean forgetting the precious memories of your loved one. You may want to seek out a Christian counselor or good friend to help you work through your grief. The good news is your loved one would not want you to stay stuck in grief and bitterness. A fresh start is moving forward with the loved one in your heart into a better season of life.

BITTER TOWARD GOD

Have you ever looked toward heaven and said something like, "God, why are you letting this happen to me? Why are you allowing these difficulties?" At some point in our life, we have probably all blamed God for the circumstances in our life. The Bible teaches us that "God is not the author of evil or confusion" (1 Cor. 14:33; see also James 3:14–16). In fact, the Bible says quite the opposite: "For I know the thoughts that I think toward you, says the LORD, thoughts of peace and not of evil, to give you a future and a hope" (Jer. 29:11). Where we get confused is in our understanding of the source of our problem. I am not here to give a religious explanation as to *why* bad things happen to good people. There are some questions that may never be answered until we get to heaven. However, we can recognize a few sources of where our problems are coming from.

The first possible reason for our difficulties may be the result of living in a fallen world. We experience devastating sicknesses, economic hardships, and many other circumstances that impact our lives. We can turn to God in these difficulties and He promises to see us through.

Another possible reason bad things come into our lives, for which we might blame God, is because of the poor choices of others. We mistakenly blame God for a variety of bad decisions others have made. A family member of mine no longer goes to church or has a relationship with God because his father, a former pastor, fell back into alcoholism and the church closed. This family member is bitter toward God because of the decisions of his father. He is placing blame on God for *not doing something* when it was his father that made the poor choices. Another example of this is of a friend of mine had a very sick child and there was little the doctors could do for him. I tried to tell him to get his son prayed for in church and to seek God for healing. His response to me was that he no longer went to church because he saw the "church leadership" make corrupt decisions. This man is keeping his family out of relationship with God because of the bad decisions of a church leadership.

The third reason difficulties can come our way, for which we might blame God, is because of our own sin and poor choices. When I became very sick, I repeatedly said to God, "Why are *You* allowing this to happen to me?" I didn't realize at the time; but that sickness was the result of many things, some of which were my own poor choices. *The beauty of our trials is that God can bring correction into our lives so that we never have to face those same consequences again.* We don't often like to think of God as being a good Father who needs to correct us now and again, but this is scriptural:

> For whom the LORD loves He corrects, Just as a father the son in whom he delights.
>
> —PROVERBS 3:12

The fourth reason negative things come our way is because of spiritual attacks. Sometimes negative things come into our lives simply because the devil is fighting us.

I remember when I was getting ready to speak at a women's conference. It was two days before the conference, and I was beginning to pack and go over my notes. That day as I was preparing, I turned and threw out my lower back. I didn't turn in an unusual way, I was simply moving about like I always do and the muscles in my lower back tightened. I was in excruciating pain. I could barely walk, and to sit down or stand up brought tremendous pain.

I could have blamed God and got mad at Him for allowing this to happen, but I didn't. I actually got very happy because I knew something good was going to happen at this conference if the devil was fighting me this hard. The topic that I was going to be speaking on was on generational curses and sexual sin. I knew that women would get set free and the devil was working overtime to prevent me from going.

As it turned out, I went moving very slowly. Right before I went up to preach, I said a simple prayer to God. I asked Him for His strength to help me deliver His message. By the time I got done preaching and praying for people, the severe pain was gone and it got better and better from that point on. When we are tempted to blame God, step back and attempt to identify the source. God does not treat us harshly; in fact, we can learn and grow from the adversities we overcome.

GREAT BITTERNESS

There can be great purpose in great bitterness. Hezekiah king of Judah was sick unto death. He cried out to the Lord. He stated his predicament and the sorrow of his heart before God. (See Isaiah 38:9–15.) Below is an excerpt chronicling his sickness *and recovery*:

> O Lord, by these things men live; And in all these things is the life of my spirit; So You will restore me and make me live. *Indeed it was for my own peace That I had great bitterness*; But You have lovingly delivered my soul from the pit of corruption, For You have cast all my sins behind Your back. For Sheol cannot thank You, Death cannot praise You; Those who go down to the pit cannot hope for Your truth. The living, the living man, he shall praise You, As I do this day.
> —Isaiah 38:16–21, emphasis added

Hezekiah was sick unto death, but God healed him and extended his life. Notice that Hezekiah said, "It was for my own peace that I had great bitterness."

God is not the author of our pain; but while we are in that pain God can strip away our selfish, prideful, and fearful attitudes.

I was not the same person after I recovered from my illness. By the time the illness was over, I felt like God did surgery on my character and surgery on my heart. He stripped away mindsets and attitudes that were causing me harm. I wasn't even aware of the harm these toxic mindsets were causing me, but they were making me sick.

Even now as I write this, I sense that there are some of you that have been through your own great bitterness and the Holy Spirit wants you to know that *the place of your pain will become the place of your anointing, the place of your strength.* Better days are ahead of you!

> Nothing *is* better for a man *than* that he should eat and drink, and *that his soul* should enjoy good in his labor. This also, I saw, was from the hand of God.
> —Ecclesiastes 2:24, emphasis added

When you're tempted to get bitter toward God, understand that His heart toward you is good. When we fall into bitterness towards God, we are separating ourselves from the only One who can truly help us. Restoration is always God's goal when our hearts are turned toward Him. He is for us and not against us (Rom. 8:31).

Below is a prayer to release anger and bitterness.

Prayer

God, I want to be free from all anger and bitterness. I no longer want to give place to the anger and bitterness in my heart. I release to You all the people (and at times even You) who I have been angry and bitter with. I want to be cleansed of the offenses that I have carried in the deep recesses of my heart. I ask You to forgive me for my anger and bitterness. And forgive me for thinking I needed to see justice before I could forgive. I now look forward to the fresh start and new beginnings that You have planned for my future. In Jesus' name I pray. Amen.

Chapter 11

UNFORGIVENESS

ORGIVENESS IS TWOFOLD: first it is accepting the forgiveness God gives to us; and secondly, it is forgiving those who have offended us. Accepting forgiveness for yourself and lending forgiveness to others is essential to our emotional and physical health. In this chapter we will be looking at forgiveness in two areas: (1) the ability to forgive others, and (2) the ability to forgive ourselves. Both are equally important, and both will imprison us if we choose not to forgive. Holding on to unforgiveness, whether it's unforgiveness toward ourselves or unforgiveness towards others, is like ingesting a poison into our body. Our sins and the sins that have been committed against us keep us stuck in emotional and physical bondage. The good news is that Jesus hands us the keys of forgiveness to set us free.

FORGIVING OTHERS

> Bearing with one another and forgiving one another…even as Christ forgave you, so you also must do.
> —COLOSSIANS 3:13

Perhaps you don't see the harm in staying angry at the person who hurt you, or perhaps you want to see the person get what's coming to them (at least a little bit). Maybe you've tried talking with the person who hurt you and the conversation went nowhere. Or, if the person who hurt you is deceased, you may think forgiveness isn't necessary. Whatever your views on forgiveness are, I hope to present to you the importance of practicing forgiveness.

The Bible teaches us to forgive. In fact, when Jesus taught us how to pray the Lord's Prayer, He said pray to God this way, "Forgive us our debts, As we forgive our debtors" (Matt. 6:12). There is symmetry between us receiving forgiveness from God and us extending forgiveness to others. Notice Jesus said, "Forgive us…, *as we* forgive our debtors." There is a connection between what we receive from God and what we give out to other people.

I will show in just a moment, in the Gospel of Matthew chapter 18, God's perspective on the importance of forgiving others. Jesus was so serious about forgiveness that after He concluded the Lord's Prayer, He goes right back to the issue of forgiveness: He says, "For if you forgive men their trespasses, your heavenly Father will also forgive you. But if you do not forgive men their trespasses, neither will your Father forgive your trespasses" (Matt. 6:14–15).There is a condition to God forgiving us; that condition is us forgiving others.

In the Gospel of John we read that after the Resurrection Jesus appeared to the disciples and He said four things to them; one of which was, "If you forgive the sins of any, they are forgiven them; if you retain the sins of any, they are retained" (John 20:23). I was intrigued by this scripture because of the word *retain* that is used. The first part of this verse says if you forgive someone they are forgiven, but if you retain some else's sins they are retained.

According to *Merriam-Webster*, the word *retain* means, "to keep in possession, to keep in mind and memory, to hold secure and intact." I thought. "Why is it so hard for us to forgive and why do we choose many times to "retain" others' sins? Why do we want to hold securely someone else's offenses against us?" The root of the Greek word translated *retain* means to be ruler or master of. When we refuse to forgive someone and we "retain" their sins, we think we have power over them or are master of the hurtful situation. What a powerful revelation! There are times when we won't forgive because holding onto our unforgiveness gives us a false sense of power.

The truth is, as we choose to not release the other person for their offense *we are not released*. Remember, Jesus said, "But if you do not forgive men their trespasses, neither will your Father forgive your trespasses" (Matt. 6:15). And if we do not find forgiveness with our heavenly Father, we are stuck in emotional and physical afflictions.

Let's keep studying Jesus' teaching on unforgiveness. In Matthew chapter 18 Jesus teaches on forgiveness in a parable. This parable changed my life and forever changed my perspective on the issue of forgiveness.

> Then Peter came to Him and said, "Lord, how often shall my brother sin against me, and I forgive him? Up to seven times?" Jesus said to him, "I do not say to you, up to seven times, but up to seventy times seven. Therefore the kingdom of heaven is like a certain king [God] who wanted to settle accounts with his servants [us]. And when he had begun to settle accounts, one was brought to him who owed him ten thousand talents. But as he was not able to pay, his master commanded that he be sold, with his wife and children and all that he had, and that payment be made. The servant [us] therefore fell down before him, saying, 'Master, have patience with me, and I will pay you

all.' Then the master [God] of that servant was moved with compassion, *released him, and forgave him the debt.*"

—Matthew 18:21–27, emphasis added

In this first part of the parable, we learn what God does for us when He forgives us. The passage says God is moved with compassion towards us. God knows that humanity commits sins out of *our foolish pride, our own hurts,* or *our ignorance.* God knows the "why" behind our actions and words, and yet He still chooses to have compassion on us and forgive us. This parable in Matthew 18 is telling us that God releases and forgives us; but what exactly do these two words mean us?

The word *release* carries the connotation of a prisoner who has been released from jail, a captive who is loosed of his bonds. We learn that God releases us from the price of our sins and past mistakes. When we sin, there is a debt that we owe—there is a price to pay for our sin. God can release us from our debt because Jesus already paid our debt of sin on the cross. To be released from our sin takes the weight of sin off our emotions and body.

The second thing we learn is that God forgives us. The word *forgive* carries the connotation of to divorce or to send away. God literally divorces us from our sin. When we receive God's forgiveness, the sin that was stuck to us like Velcro has to leave us. Both words, *release* and *forgive,* share a common root meaning—to separate. When we are released and forgiven from our sins, we are separated from our sin. The union that we once shared with sin is now destroyed when we come to God and are truly repentant for our sin. In the eyes of God we are no longer attached to our sin, we are released and set free from what we have done wrong. This negates any label we have put on ourselves as being "a bad person."

Let's go a little deeper. Everyone has a conscious; we know the difference between good and evil, between right and wrong. When we violate our conscious and we sin with our mouth, thoughts, or actions, there is a sense of guilt and shame that come to join our life. Once we sin and are under guilt and shame, we are now tormented by the wrong we have just said or done. Our body, through the hypothalamus gland, is reacting to the weight of our wrongdoing.[1] If we aren't able to find a way to release our guilt and shame we may become sick in mind or body as a result.

So, how do we get free from our burden of sin and all that comes along with it? The answer is simple yet powerful: we find rest from our souls and freedom from our sins when we go to God ask Him to forgive us from our wrongdoings. God has compassion on us and removes the weight of our sin. Our sin and wrongdoing have been lifted from us.

But there is just one catch: once again remembering that Jesus said: "But if you do not forgive men their trespasses, neither will your Father forgive your trespasses" (Matt. 6:15). This infers the answer to the question, why is it so important that we forgive others? It's because when we give forgiveness to others, we reap the benefit of forgiveness in our own life.

Let's read the rest of the parable from Matthew 18. To recap so far, the man owed a large debt, the king (God) had compassion on the man and forgave him his debt. In the second part of this parable the man who had his debt wiped clean by the king is now confronted with someone who owes him. Let's find out what this newly forgiven man does when confronted with the issue of lending forgiveness to someone else.

> [Jesus continued,] "But that servant went out and found one of *his fellow servants* [those who have sinned against us] who owed him a hundred denarii; and he laid hands on him and took him by the throat, saying, 'Pay me what you owe!' So his fellow servant fell down at his feet and begged him, saying, 'Have patience with me, and I will pay you all.' And he would not, but went and threw him into prison till he should pay the debt. So when his fellow servants saw what had been done, they were very grieved, and came and told their master [God] all that had been done. Then his master, after he had called him, said to him [us], 'You wicked servant! I forgave you all that debt because you begged me. Should you not also have had compassion on your fellow servant, just as I had pity on you?' And his master was angry, and *delivered him to the torturers* until he should pay all that was due to him. So My heavenly Father also will do to you if each of you, from his heart, does not forgive his brother his trespasses."
> —MATTHEW 18:28–35, EMPHASIS ADDED

The man who had just received compassion and forgiveness from God for his debt refuses to forgive someone else's debt that is owed to him. The man chose not to lend that same forgiveness to his fellow man. The man who chose not to forgive someone else was released to the *torturers*. And to drive this point home even further, Jesus ends the parable with: "So My heavenly Father also will do to you if each of you, from his heart, does not forgive." These are powerful words spoken by the One who understands the principles of unforgiveness.

I have had the torturers released in my life because of unforgiveness, and I never want to be that foolish again. I will be sharing that story in just a moment. But before I do, let's look at the word *torturers* in the original Greek. *Torturers* in this version is translated *tormentors* in some versions. The root word means to jail, to vex with grievous pain in the mind or body, to harass, and to distress. When we don't forgive, the parable teaches us that *we* (not the other person) will be vexed, have pain in the mind or body, or be distressed. This truth is enough to make us look at our life and see who we still need to forgive.

We can be like that unforgiving man in the parable. God forgives us of our debt whether great or small and when someone sins against us we refuse to forgive them. Remember, we all sin out of *our pride, our hurt,* or *our foolishness.* Shouldn't we have the same compassion on others that God gives us?

After all this teaching on forgiveness, you may still be left saying, "But what about the person who hurt me or abused me? Am I supposed to pretend like nothing ever happened?" No. This is where we get stuck and stay stuck for weeks, months, years, or even decades. We may say, "If you only you knew what they did to me and how they messed up my life, then you would understand why they don't deserve forgiveness." When we think this way we feel justified in our unforgiveness. In some cases we feel deeply betrayed because the person who hurt us is someone we dearly loved and trusted. The closer the person is to us, the more emotional pain we may experience.

We may feel like we don't want to be around that person any longer; and yet if it's a family member we may have no choice but to see that person often. I have had this experience with a family member. The first option is always to go to the person and discuss hurt feelings and discuss ways to restore the relationship. If the person is not willing to restore the relationship and has a condescending attitude toward you, then you still need to forgive and release that person. You can keep a healthy distance from that person to prevent you from getting hurt by them again.

You're not going to change the other person. But you are responsible to look at areas of your life that may need some changing. Many times I've gone to God and asked Him to clean up my own heart. I don't try and play God and figure out the consequences the other person should get for hurting me. It is our responsibility to forgive the person that hurt us, and it is *God's responsibility* to be the Judge over that person. We are instructed to forgive, not to punish or take revenge. We are not God, nor do we want His job. There is that principle that says what a person has sown that he shall also reap (Gal. 6:7).

In cases where it is a spouse that has wounded you or betrayed you, particularly in cases of adultery, humility and honesty are greatly needed. If restoration of the marriage is the goal, then the spouse who cheated and broke trust will need to rebuild that trust with their spouse. The spouse that cheated will need to reassure and be very tender towards the hurting spouse. The spouse who was cheated on is now wounded, and it will take the patience and faithfulness of the cheating spouse to rebuild the hurt spouse's confidence in them. If the two people cannot come together and forgive and rebuild the trust that has been lost, then a third party, perhaps a counselor, is needed.

Whether it's in a marriage or any other relationship, we always need to lend forgiveness. As we recount the above parable, we don't want to be stubborn and refuse to forgive because we open *ourselves* up to the tormentors being released in our life.

As you look back on your life and you see the mistakes you made, aren't you glad you were able to learn and grow from your mistakes? At the time you made those mistakes, you probably didn't realize those mistakes may have wounded others along the way. I would say to you that there is a good chance the person who has hurt you and offended you doesn't understand the full capacity and consequences of how they hurt you. In fact, it is very likely that they hurt you because somewhere along the way they have been hurt. That doesn't make what they did right, but it does bring some understanding as to why they hurt you. Recognizing this truth allows us to lend forgiveness.

When Jesus was crucified on the cross, He looked up to heaven and said, "Father, forgive them, for they do not know what they do" (Luke 23:34). None of us have been crucified on a cross by others, although at times it may feel like we have; nonetheless, we should follow Jesus' example by forgiving our offenders and leaving their judgment up to God.

Some of you still may have a bit of a dilemma here because on the one hand you know what God commands you to do—forgive—and yet on the other hand you are still having a hard time letting the offense go. To shed more light on the subject of forgiving others, it's important to understand what it means when we *choose* to forgive. Focus on the Family published an article on forgiveness that reveals *truths on forgiveness* that are important to understand the process of forgiving. Here is a portion of that article:

> **Forgiveness is not letting the offender off the hook.** We can and should still hold others accountable for their actions or lack of actions.
>
> **Forgiveness is returning to God the right to take care of justice.** By refusing to transfer the right to exact punishment or revenge, we are telling God we don't trust him to take care of matters.
>
> **Forgiveness is not letting the offense recur again and again.** We don't have to tolerate, nor should we keep ourselves open to, lack of respect or any form of abuse.
>
> **Forgiveness does not mean we have to revert to being the victim.** Forgiving is not saying, "What you did was okay, so go ahead and walk all over me."
>
> **Forgiveness is not the same as reconciling.** We can forgive someone even if we never get along with them again…
>
> **We have to forgive every time.** If we find ourselves constantly

forgiving, though, we might need to take a look at the dance we are doing with the other person that sets us up to be continually hurt, attacked, or abused.

Forgetting does not mean denying reality or ignoring repeated offenses. Some people are obnoxious, mean-spirited, apathetic, or unreliable. They never will change. We need to change the way we respond to them and quit expecting them to be different.

If they don't repent, we still have to forgive. Even if they never ask, we need to forgive. We should memorize and repeat over and over: Forgiveness is about our attitude, not their action.[2]

This article explained that we are all a work in progress and many times forgiving someone may take time and a determined effort on our part. But it's important to remember the dividend that forgiveness pays in our life and in the lives of others. We are next going to discuss when we need to lend forgiveness *to ourselves*.

Forgiving Ourselves

> Bless the LORD, O my soul, And forget not all His benefits: Who *forgives* all [my] iniquities, Who heals all [my] diseases.
> —Psalm 103:2–3, emphasis added

Sometimes the hardest person to forgive is ourselves. Maybe for some forgiving others is a difficult task; but there are others, myself included, that have had a difficult time forgiving ourselves. When we feel we cannot forgive ourselves, it's because we believe there is still a price we need to pay or a punishment that we still deserve.

I remember praying for a woman at a conference; I began to say to her, "The blood of Jesus is enough; the blood of Jesus is enough." And before I was able to make sense of what was happening, this woman began to weep and cry. She was being set free from unforgiveness towards herself. God wanted her to know that Jesus' shed blood on the cross was a sufficient price for her wrongdoing *and* that her sin *was already paid* for. With this realization she could be free from the weight of sin, shame, and condemnation that she carried. It's this truth that I have to remind myself of in times when I feel I need to pay a price for the wrong that I have done. The cross of Jesus was enough for my sin and yours.

Separate from the mistake

Getting free begins with separating ourselves from our sin. By this I mean that we need to realize that when *we make a mistake, we* (as a person) *are not a mistake*. At times *we fail*, but that *does not mean we are a failure*. Our identity is not defined by our wrongdoings. There is a big difference. You may need to go back and reread those first few statements. You are not the sum result of your mistakes.

In order to recover from our sin we have to be able to separate our identity from our mistakes. This is similar to when a child misbehaves. The child does something wrong, but the parent still loves that child. Even though the child has misbehaved, the child is still valued in the eyes of the parent. The healthy parent can separate the child from the bad choice the child made. The parent sees the potential for that child to grow beyond their bad behavior.

God sees the potential in us and He knows we can learn, grow, and move beyond our mistakes. In Isaiah 1:18 we read what God says about our mistakes:

> "Come now, and let us reason together," Says the LORD, "Though our sins are like scarlet, They shall be as white as snow; Though they are red like crimson, They shall be as wool."
>
> —ISAIAH 1:18

If you are still struggling with sin and guilt, this is a scripture that you may want to put in your home—maybe on the refrigerator or a mirror. Read this scripture over and over again until this truth sinks into your heart. By reading scriptures like this, you are creating a new mindset, a godly mindset that your guilt and sins can be washed clean.

Jesus went to a place called Golgotha and hung on a wooden cross and gave His sinless life for our sinful condition. That is love and that is freedom. The cross frees us from all our mistakes, wrong choices, and sins.

I'm going to share a powerful testimony on what can happen to a person when they hold unforgiveness against themselves.

The three-month ordeal

There is a hidden weapon that the devil uses against us and that is *unforgiveness toward ourselves*. The best way to illustrate the damage that unforgiveness towards ourselves can bring is to share my experience in this area.

There was a time in my life when every time I took a bite of food I thought I was going to choke and die. This went on for about three months. Every breakfast, every lunch, and every dinner I was tormented by the thought that I was going to die because I believed food would get stuck in my throat and I would not be able to breathe. This was an extremely tormenting time. I did eat during this time, but it was very little and I lost a lot of weight. This became very dangerous to me physically because without proper food we open ourselves up to sickness. The devil knew this and was having a field day with me.

Finally after about three months of living this way, my sister-in-law knew of a missionary couple that was going to be visiting our church. Missionary couples often see many bondages and torments and see people set free by the power of God. My sister-in-law suggested that the missionary's wife pray for me. We set up the meeting and the missionary's wife and my sister-in-law began to pray for me. During the prayer, the missionary stopped, looked up at me, and said, "*You need to forgive yourself for an abortion you had.*" I was startled and shocked! This woman did not know anything about me or my past, and she certainly had no way of knowing about the abortion. I knew God revealed this to her to help me get free.

I was harboring unforgiveness towards myself for the abortion; and the fear of choking and dying was a form of punishment I felt I deserved. Incidentally this new "fear" began soon after the birth of my first child. You see, by me having my new born baby, I subconsciously realized what I "gave up" by having the abortion. When I was holding my firstborn, the realization hit me that if I had not committed the abortion I would have had another child. There was a wound in my soul, and the way it was surfacing was through this fear that began right after I delivered my first child.

The missionary's wife led me through a prayer of forgiveness towards myself. The next morning I woke up and the fear of choking was gone. It has been twenty years since that prayer, and I have not experienced the fear of choking since that time.

I tell you of this experience to show you how unforgiveness toward ourselves can keep us tormented and in bondage. The interesting thing is, if a psychiatrist got a hold of me there is a good chance they would have put me on medication and labeled me with an illness. I did not have any illness, I had an unforgiveness problem. I did not need medication, I needed a heart wound to be healed. I did not need years of therapy, I needed to be free of unforgiveness toward myself. This makes me wonder how many people have various "issues" who just need to be healed from such toxic emotions as unforgiveness.

As I have said, unforgiveness gives the devil an open door into our lives. It gives the devil an opportunity to torment us. I would advise you to ask the Holy Spirit to reveal to you if there are any areas of your life that you are holding onto unforgiveness toward yourself. Unforgiveness is a toxic emotion that the devil uses to gain a foothold into our lives. We are susceptible to these toxic emotions because of the hurts that lie dormant in our lives. These hurts lie dormant for months, even years, and manifest themselves in a variety of ways. These hurts need to be brought into the light. The worst thing we can do is to keep our hurts hidden in the secret places of our hearts. Perhaps you may want to talk to a good friend or Christian counselor or journal about these areas and then pray and release your wrongdoings to God.

Unforgiveness and Sickness

I have shared my personal testimony of the relationship between sin and sickness, but we also find this principle in the Book of Isaiah. For some of us there can be a connection between our sins and our sickness. Isaiah 53:5 teaches us this truth.

> But He was wounded for our transgressions, He was bruised for our iniquities; The chastisement of our peace was upon Him, And by His stripes we are healed.
> —Isaiah 53:5

If we break this scripture down in the original Hebrew language, we learn that Jesus traded His divinity to save humanity. Study closely the breakdown below.

- [Jesus] was *wounded* for our *transgressions*.
    Definition of *wounded*—defiled, dishonored, and became weak
    Definition of *transgression*—offenses, rebellion, and faults

- He was *bruised* for our *iniquities*.
    Definition of *bruised*—to crush into pieces, to bend, to twist, to shatter, and to oppress
    Definition of *iniquities*—perversity and wickedness

If we tie these definitions together, we learn that Jesus became defiled, dishonored, and crushed because of our offenses and wickedness. He did this to provide our freedom from our sin.

Let's look at the last part of this verse. I like how the Living Bible translates this portion of the verse:

> He was beaten that we might have peace; he was lashed—and we were healed!
> —Isaiah 53:5, TLB

It is clear that Jesus took our punishment for us and gave us healing. For years I spoke the second half of verse 5, saying, "By Your stripes I am healed," and I saw little results. I was not accepting the first part of verse 5, that He was wounded for my sins and bruised for my iniquities. I can't keep my sin and guilt and expect to be healed. I will say that again: you can't keep your sin and guilt and expect to be healed. We can't hang onto our sin, live with our sin, beat ourselves up for our sin, and expect to be healed and healthy. Many times we cry out to God for healing, we get scriptures on healing, and we have faith that we will be healed; yet we remain in our thoughts of sin, shame, guilt, and condemnation.

To sum up this scripture, Jesus became weak in exchange for our offenses and Jesus was crushed and oppressed for our sin and wrongdoings. And because Jesus went through all of this, this scripture says we are healed.

Why would He do all of this? Why would He leave heaven to come to earth to endure hell? The answer is a simple, yet a serious one. The answer is because of His great love for you and me. His death signifies the emancipation of the human spirit, soul, and body. Jesus set us free from sin and all that sin brings with it. Realizing and accepting what He did is one of the keys to getting free. *Not accepting His forgiveness is like telling Him the cross was not enough.*

JESUS FORGIVES SINS AND HEALING OCCURS

Jesus' ability to forgive results in freedom from emotional and physical sicknesses. We are going to look at two examples from scripture where Jesus forgave a person and the person gained emotional or physical health.

The paralytic

The first account is of a man who was a paralytic:

> Then behold, they brought to Him a paralytic lying on a bed. When Jesus saw their faith, He said to the paralytic, "Son, be of good cheer; your sins are forgiven you."
> —MATTHEW 9:2

A *paralytic* is someone who is unable to move or feel part of their body or a state of being unable to function, act, or move. This man had a serious physical affliction. In scripture we learn the paralyzed man was brought to Jesus by his friends. Jesus "saw *their* faith," the faith of the man's friends. Jesus recognized and was pleased with their faith. We know this because the Bible says it's impossible to please God without faith (Heb. 11:6). So, this paralyzed man is brought before Jesus. The friends' faith got the man to Jesus, but now Jesus is going to do a deeper work in the man's heart.

The first word that Jesus said to this man was "son." Jesus calls him son. Think about that for a moment; the word *son* indicates endearment. When someone calls you son or daughter, it shows your identity, your connection to the person. The next thing that Jesus says to him is, "Be of good cheer." This means to have courage, have confidence. Jesus was easing this man's fears. Jesus was saying, "Be of good courage, be of good cheer; you are about to be released from your sins and affliction." Jesus knew that being released from his sins would result in being released from his paralysis. In the presence of Jesus, something good was about to happen to this man.

Some of you need to get into the presence of Jesus and pour out the areas of unforgiveness that are in your heart. The Holy Spirit wants to assure you that, just like the man in this text, you can be of good cheer and take courage because your sins can be forgiven and your emotional and physical health can be recovered.

Jesus continued on with this man. After some resistance from the religious leaders, Jesus said to the paralytic man, "Arise, take up your bed, and go to your house" (Matt. 9:6). Jesus first pronounced him *forgiven* (v. 2) and next declared to him to *arise, take up his bed, and go home* (v. 6). *Arise* means to arouse from sleep and to collect one's faculties. Do you see Jesus forgave the man *and then* healed the man? There are times when forgiveness must come first and then our healing.

We get so accustomed to our current situation of emotional or physical sickness that it takes the faith of a few friends and a word of Jesus to wake us up from our current situation. We need to awaken to the realization that God desires to heal our hearts. The Bible does not tell us what kind of sins this man was forgiven of; we just learn that this man needed his soul cleansed from the weight of his sins. Once the burden of his sins was removed, he received his physical healing.

The woman of sin

The next scripture we are going to look at is of a woman who led a life of much sin. She is the women who washed the feet of Jesus with her tears. This woman loved much because she was forgiven for much.

> And behold, a woman in the city who was a sinner, when she knew that Jesus sat at the table in the Pharisee's house, brought an alabaster flask of fragrant oil, and stood at His feet behind Him weeping; and she began to wash His feet with her tears, and wiped them with the hair of her head; and she kissed His feet and anointed them with the fragrant oil. Now when the Pharisee who had invited Him saw this, he spoke to himself, saying, "This Man, if He were a prophet, would know who and what manner of woman this is who is touching Him, for she is a sinner." And Jesus answered and said to him, "Simon, I have something to say to you." So he said, "Teacher, say it." "There was a certain creditor who had two debtors. One owed five hundred denarii, and the other fifty. And when they had nothing with which to repay, he freely forgave them both. Tell Me, therefore, which of them will love him more?" Simon answered and said, "I suppose the one whom he forgave more." And He said to him, "You have rightly judged." Then He turned to the woman and said to Simon, "Do you see this woman? I entered your house; you

gave Me no water for My feet, but she has washed My feet with her tears and wiped them with the hair of her head. You gave Me no kiss, but this woman has not ceased to kiss My feet since the time I came in. You did not anoint My head with oil, but this woman has anointed My feet with fragrant oil. Therefore I say to you, her sins, which are many, are forgiven, for she loved much. But to whom little is forgiven, the same loves little." Then He said to her, "*Your sins are forgiven.*" And those who sat at the table with Him began to say to themselves, "Who is this who even forgives sins?" Then He said to the woman, "Your faith has saved you. *Go in peace.*"

—Luke 7:37–50, emphasis added

This woman had a reputation. She was known for her sin. We gather that her sin may have been sexual because the Pharisee says if Jesus were a prophet He "would know who and what manner of woman this is who is touching Him, for she is a sinner." Her guilt and shame must have been apparent because the Pharisee knew "what manner of woman" she was.

We observe this woman's remorse because the Bible says, she was weeping and she began to wash his feet with her tears. The weight of her sin and regret must have been heavy. Jesus was well aware of what kind of woman she was, but He was more aware that her soul was in desperate need of cleansing. Just like this woman, Jesus is aware of our past mistakes and He knows that what our soul needs is to be cleansed.

He says to her, "Your sins are forgiven… Your faith has saved you. Go in peace." The word translated *forgiven* means to separate in the original Greek. You see, Jesus was separating her from her sin. He wants to do the same thing for us. We no longer have to be identified with our sin. We no longer have to carry the burden of sin and wrongdoings. When we ask for forgiveness, Jesus cleanses us from our past; He separates us from our past. He then says to her, "Your faith has saved you. Go in peace." The Greek word translated "peace" means the exemption from the rage and havoc of war. You see, when we are carrying our sin, our emotions and physical body is at war. Just like this woman, Jesus tells us we are forgiven and to be in peace, the war is over with our past. We can let our past go and begin anew.

In Conclusion

Please understand that we are not perfect nor will we will achieve perfection until we get to heaven. We have all had experiences where we wish we could take back something we said or did. So how do we get over this? How do we let go of our sin and unforgiveness?

First, go to God and pour out your heart to Him in prayer, asking Him to forgive you and cleanse you. If it's a weakness in your life, ask Him for wisdom and courage to be changed in this area. Secondly, if the mistake involves hurting someone's feelings, we can go to them with a repentant heart and apologize for the wrong that we did. Most people, when they see your repentant heart, will lend forgiveness to you. If they don't, then that is between them and God, you've done your part. There are some cases where it is not possible to go the other person; in such cases you may want to write a letter to that person explaining why you did what you did. Then you *need to forgive yourself.* It is the process of identifying the unforgiveness that is in our heart, then doing what we know to do to make things right, and then forgiving others or forgiving ourselves.

Prayer to forgive someone else

Below is a prayer that will help you on your journey of forgiving what others have done to you. You may want to mark this page and come back to this prayer if you feel you're struggling with forgiving someone. This prayer can also be found in chapter 14 of this book. You may have to repeat this prayer for a couple of days or even a couple of weeks as you work through the pain that person has caused you.

> *Dear heavenly Father, You see the wound in my heart this person has caused me. You know all the reasons behind their actions. Today I make the choice to forgive them. God, I release this person into Your hands. I will not seek revenge upon them for their actions but I pray Your mercy in their life. I pray You would cleanse and restore my mind, my body, and my spirit from their offense. Thank You that You have heard my prayer and that You are faithful to restore my joy and peace back to me. In Jesus' name I pray. Amen.*

Prayer to forgive yourself

As with the prayer to forgive others, you may want to mark this page in your book. There may be several times when you have to come to this prayer to be released from unforgiveness toward yourself. I would also encourage you to say this prayer out loud. Our brain is more apt to believe the words that come out of our mouth. That is why the words we speak over our lives are so important.

> *God, I admit my wrongdoing and my mistake, I shouldn't have done what I did. I'm going to lay my sin at Your cross. I am going to learn from this experience and accept the forgiveness that You desire to give to*

me. Jesus, I thank You that Your blood will cover my sin and my shame. God, if I have caused anyone pain or hurt, I pray that Your Holy Spirit will minster life and peace to that person or that situation. God, I accept Your mercy and forgiveness and I now choose to forgive myself. Once again, I now choose to forgive myself. I no longer will see myself or get my identity from my mistakes. I thank You for the new beginnings You have in store for my life. In Jesus' name I pray. Amen.

Once you have prayed the prayer, you have to discipline your mind not to keep thinking about the wrongdoing. If the thought of your past mistakes or other's offenses keep coming up, then write some scriptures down on an index card that pertain to forgiveness and put them where you will read them each day. Below are scriptures that pertain to forgiveness:

- He has thrown my sins as far as the east is to the west (Ps. 103:12).
- He has thrown my sins in depths of the sea (Micah 7:19).
- "Blessed is he whose transgression is forgiven, Whose sin is covered" (Ps. 32:1).
- "For You, Lord, are good, and ready to forgive, And abundant in mercy to all those who call upon You" (Ps. 86:5).
- "Then He answered and spoke to those who stood before Him, saying, 'Take away the filthy garments from him.' And to him He said, 'See, I have removed your iniquity from you, and I will clothe you with rich robes'" (Zech. 3:4).
- "And you, being dead in your trespasses and the uncircumcision of your flesh, He has made alive together with Him, having forgiven you all trespasses" (Col. 2:13).
- "In Him we have redemption through His blood, the forgiveness of sins, according to the riches of His grace" (Eph. 1:7)
- "If we confess our sins, He is faithful and just to forgive us our sins and to cleanse us from all unrighteousness" (1 John 1:9).
- "I write to you, little children, Because your sins are forgiven you for His name's sake" (1 John 2:12).

Part 3

Continuing to Overcome

Chapter 12
YOUR RELATIONSHIP WITH GOD

For emotional health to be achieved, having a close relationship with God *is essential*. He is the architect of who we are, so it would make sense that we seek Him for our wholeness. It's important to know God as the Father, the Son (Jesus), and as the Holy Spirit. There is one God who functions in three distinct roles.

Someone once gave me an example to understand the Trinity. One man can be a father to his children, a husband to his wife, and an employee to his employer; yet he is still one man. This one man functions in different roles but he is still the same man. It's the same way with God. God is one God, but functions as God the Father, God the Son, and God the Holy Spirit.

The *Father* represents our provider, our supplier, our source. He is the engineer and the designer of our lives. He is the Creator of all things. He is from everlasting to everlasting. And He is love.

Jesus represents our Redeemer, our Savior from sin, our Advocate. He is our way maker, our Prince of Peace, our rescuer, and our best friend. Jesus *is* the image of God for us.

The *Holy Spirit* represents our Counselor, our comfort, and our consoler. He is the arm of God on the earth. He encourages us, strengthens us, and gives us revelation of who Jesus Christ is. He is our wisdom giver, the one who convicts us of sin, and the one who leads us into all truth. An entire book could be written on the attributes of the triune God. The important thing to remember is that as great and magnificent as God is, He desires a personal relationship with you and me.

HEART KNOWLEDGE VS HEAD KNOWLEDGE

It took me a long time to believe *in my heart* that God was a personal God. I had a basic understanding that God was awesome and powerful, but I didn't know He was personally interested in my life. One morning, over breakfast, I shared with my husband how I finally understood in my heart God's personal love for me. I was explaining to him that my relationship with God was more than a bunch of Sunday school stories that I learned as a child. God was real to me. My relationship to God was not a regurgitation of John 3:16, but I finally had a deep heart revelation that He loved me.

The evening after I told my husband of my new found confidence in God's love for me, we had a church service. When worship began God spoke to my heart; He communicated to me that He was pleased that my doubts about Him had been resolved. It was as though God was happy that I knew He loved me. Think about that for a moment; the God of heaven wants you and me to be secure in His love for us.

In the past I viewed God through the example of other people, but people are imperfect and can disappoint us. This is unfair to view God based on how a church or a pastor has treated us. It's also unfair to view God through our disappointments. None of the above will give us an accurate view of God.

He says about Himself in the Book of Hosea, "I am God, and not man... And I will not come with terror" (11:9). God is not the angry gray-haired man sitting on a throne in heaven waiting to zap us. It's quite the opposite. When we turn to God and confess our mistakes, He is waiting with grace and mercy to restore us. God desires a friendship with us. God is not out for our destruction; instead He is out for our redemption.

God delights in you.

When I have felt the weight of my mistakes, God would let me know that He still delights in me. There was a time when (as much as I don't like to admit it) I got angry with God. I would say to Him, "Please forgive me for my anger, but I need five minutes to vent and be upset." There were times when I didn't understand what He was doing or how the situation was going to work out. Ironically, at the same time I was frustrated, I was already repenting to the Holy Spirit for my wrong attitude. It's because of our limited human perspective that we can't see His larger plan or greater good. It's in times like this that we ask God to have mercy on our limited perspective.

There was one such occasion when I could not see how a situation was going to work out. I opened my Bible one night before I went to sleep and my eyes fell on a scripture that seemed to leap off the page to me. (By the way, a scripture does not always jump off the page to me every time I open the Bible; but in this case it did and it was exactly what I needed in that moment.) The scripture brought tremendous peace and I was able to fall asleep because of it. The next morning when I got up and had my quiet time with God, I was opening my Bible to go to my "scheduled" reading. I was reading the Gospel of Luke. As I opened my Bible to get to Luke, I "just happened" to open my Bible to the exact same scripture that I fell asleep to eight hours before. There are about 2,000 pages in the Bible; what are the odds that I would open to the one verse that I had just read eight hours earlier. This was not a coincidence; this was the Holy Spirit getting a message to me. The scripture that I opened to is below.

> You shall no longer be termed Forsaken, Nor shall your land any more be termed Desolate; But you shall be called Hephzibah, and your land Beulah; For the LORD delights in you, And your land shall be married...And as the bridegroom rejoices over the bride, So shall your God rejoice over you.
> —ISAIAH 62:4–5

When I read this verse, the first thing that jumped out to me was that *God delighted in me*. In an instant I knew that God was not angry with me for my frustrations. I knew that whatever He was doing in my life I could rest assured it was going to turn out good. God was not mad at me for not understanding His plan or His process. He is big enough to handle our temporary frustrations. I went to sleep that night and woke up the next morning greatly encouraged because the Holy Spirit led me to this scripture.

As I continued to study this passage I found there are several important truths for us to learn. The first one is when the scripture says *we are no longer forsaken*. *Forsaken* means to be abandoned, destitute, or deserted. No matter what our past experience has been, we no longer have to walk this life alone. We have heaven on our side.

The scripture goes on to say that our "land" shall no longer be "desolate." These two words combined means devastating circumstances. The scripture says we shall *no longer* live in devastating circumstances. I would ask you what areas of your life have been devastated. It is not God's will for your life to be devastated and defeated. I believe (and I have personally experienced) that if you turn to God for wisdom and strength, He will show you the way out.

The problem is that some of us have lived in devastating circumstances for so long that the thought of walking out of those circumstances seems too good to be true. Matthew 19:26 says, "With God all things are possible."

There is a process we go through, where by God begins to turn the negative areas in our life around for good. Sometimes we are in the middle of that process and we get angry with God because we don't always see the behind-the-scenes work of the Holy Spirit in our life. At the same time God is removing areas of our life that need to go. This process can be painful, but it is necessary.

Let's continue in this verse. God says we shall be called "Hephzibah" and our land "Beulah." The name *Hephzibah* literally means my delight is in her. When God uses the word *delight* it means He is pleased with us, He favors us, and He bends down to help us. The name *Beulah* means to be married. When you put these two words together they carry connation of a good husband that delights, loves, and provides for his wife. This is the way God chooses to reveal Himself to us.

In this scripture He teaches us what relationship means to Him. In verse 5 it says, "As the bridegroom rejoices over the bride, So shall your God rejoice over you." The Bible shows us clearly that God has the same happiness towards us as the bridegroom has over his bride. God is showing us His affection toward us through the scriptures. This is why it is necessary to read the Bible to understand who God is. He invites you to learn of Him and His ways.

He has compassion for you.

I recently read the parable of the prodigal son. Most of you know the story. (See Luke 15:11–32.) A wealthy man had two sons. One of the sons went to this father and requested his inheritance early. This son took his inheritance and wasted it on "prodigal living" (v. 13). The Bible says he squandered away his inheritance on harlots and the like. The son eventually spent all his money and found himself destitute and hungry. He finally "came to himself" (v. 17) and decided to go back to his father's house and tell him, "I am no longer worthy to be called your son. Make me like one of your hired servants" (v. 19). The Bible tells us that the father saw his son returning and had compassion on him. When the father saw the son coming home, he ran to meet him and "fell on his neck and kissed him" (v. 20).

Stop for a moment and get a mental picture of what Jesus is teaching us through this parable. The father missed his son and the father longed for his son to return home. The father was so overjoyed that his son came home that he called for a celebration (vv. 22–24). We get to see a glimpse of God's very heart. We get to see the longing of the Father's heart toward us. Even in our worst state, God has tremendous love and compassion towards us.

What peace and what comfort to be in relationship with God Himself. I was contemplating how I would describe my relationship to God. I have very humbly attempted to put into words what I think of when I think of my relationship with Him.

I see a sunny day in a beautiful garden with plenty of blue skies and soft green grass. In that garden there is a gentle breeze, a lovely fragrance emanating from an assortment of colorful flowers. There is a peaceful presence of Jesus in that garden. He is strong and He is safe. His eyes are ocean blue, and His smile is as comforting as a warm sunset. There is no judgment in His eyes when He looks at me, only love. In this garden I feel secure and loved with no cares to think about, no fears to fight. Because of my relationship with Him, my days are peaceably in His hands. When I follow in His footsteps, my future is fruitful and my past mistakes are forgotten. There is a heaven, and one day I will be with God and my beloved family and friends for all of eternity in this beautiful place.

This is what my relationship to God is like. Yes, there may be sorrows and trials that we face, but if we *let Him*, He will lead us through those storms of life. Through the good times in our life and the not so good times, He is there. In times when we are praising Him for His miracles and in times when we are angry because we feel He is silent, His love still remains. He promises us to never leave us nor forsake us (Heb. 13:5).

How do we get this kind of relationship with God? It's like most relationships in our life; we have to spend time with the person. Spending time with someone enables you to get to know their character, their views, and what they value. When we spend time with someone, we learn what makes them happy and what upsets them. This kind of knowledge only comes by getting to know the person with whom you want to be close.

If you are a Christian and already have a relationship with God, there is always room to know Him more. As you daily surrender your heart to Him, inviting Him to walk with you and talk with you, He will make Himself known to you. God can speak to you in ways that will surprise you. He speaks through the Bible, through nature, or maybe through another person or through circumstances of your life. He speaks through the gentle whisper inside your heart or through a song. God has limitless ways to get your attention.

TIMES OF REFRESHING

Finding time in your day to listen for His voice is our responsibility as we pursue Him. Time to worship, pray, and read His Word are all crucial to get to know Him. What part of your day you spend with Him is up to you. The amount of time you spend with Him may vary from day to day. Some days you may have a half hour or forty-five minutes, and other days you may only have five or ten minutes. Whatever the allotted time, make sure you read His word and tell Him what's on your mind, much like you would a good friend.

My favorite part of my time with God is to find a couple of Christian worship songs and think about the words in the song. This is communicating with God and this gets your attention on Him. This time with God has become a practice of mine for over two decades. We find time for what's important to us. No matter the amount of time you start with, make *getting to know God* a priority in your life.

When we surrender our heart and soul to God, He comes to our rescue. This simple truth can change your life. The Bible says, "Repent therefore and be converted, that your sins may be blotted out, *so that times of refreshing may come from the presence of the Lord*" (Acts 3:19, emphasis added). Many of us *long* for times of refreshing. We have been carrying heavy loads for so long that we are desperate for those burdens to be lifted.

I remember years ago I was suffering from migraine headaches. One particular day I had a very painful migraine. There was a prayer meeting at church. I went. Looking back I don't know how I got there, but I did. At the prayer meeting a couple of the women in the church prayed over me that the migraine would be removed. By the end of that prayer I felt like I had spent several hours in a day spa. My head and the rest of my body felt so relaxed and refreshed. The pain was gone; and for those that have suffered from a migraine, you understand the longevity of this type of pain. This was one of those times of refreshing in the presence of God. To reject God and expect to live a life free physically, emotionally, and spiritually is incorrect. How can we operate our life without living by the owner's manual, the Bible?

How Do We Pray?

Some mornings when I'm not sure what to pray, I will refer back to the "Our Father" prayer. Some of you may be familiar with the Lord's Prayer from childhood. Jesus teaches in Matthew chapter 6 how to pray. I will reprint the prayer and then explain it further.

> Our Father in heaven, Hallowed be Your name, Your kingdom come. Your will be done On earth as it is in heaven. Give us this day our daily bread. And forgive us our debts, As we forgive our debtors. And do not lead us into temptation, But deliver us from the evil one. For Yours is the kingdom and the power and the glory forever. Amen.
> —Matthew 6:9–13

This is Jesus' perfect example of how we should pray. We can pray this prayer literally or we can say this prayer in our own words. If we choose to say this prayer literally, we need to be careful not to get into a "routine" by saying the words but not think about the meaning. Sometimes when we say a "routine prayer," our mouth is moving but our mind is someplace else. That's why it's good to pray from *your own heart* the meaning of the Lord's Prayer.

Below I have shown how the Lord's Prayer can be a guideline for us to follow.

Our Father in heaven, Hollowed be Your name.

This is an expression of praise. When we come to God we are to praise Him for who He is and what He has done in our lives. I like to play a few worship songs and sing the words back to Him and mean what I'm saying to Him. This is a form of worshiping God. You can also talk to God and tell Him how much you love and adore Him. Many times when I tell the Lord how much I love Him, whether in song or not, I feel a strong presence of the Holy Spirit.

Your kingdom come. Your will be done On earth as it is in heaven.

This is the time to pray God's perfect will for you and your family. This is when I ask God for what is in heaven to be established on earth. I often pray: "There is no sickness in heaven, there is no worry in heaven, there is no financial lack in heaven; so let it be in my life as it is in heaven." I begin to call heaven down in my home and over my husband, my children, my extended family and friends. We want to have a heavenly day, not a hellish one.

Give us this day our daily bread.

What are your needs for your day, what has been on your mind? Bring these concerns and requests to God and thank Him for making provision for you. He cares for you. Jesus said to ask, seek, and knock (Luke 11:9–13) concerning your needs. It is not God's will that you are anxious through your day. Ask Him for your daily needs to be met.

And forgive us our debts [sins], As we forgive our debtors [those who sinned against us].

This is where we can pour out our hearts to God over those areas we have fallen short. It's okay to spend time repenting over our sins, but then we need to ask for forgiveness and leave our sins at the cross. Jesus paid the price for those sins, and we do not have to go on punishing ourselves for our past mistakes.

The second part of this verse is to extend the same forgiveness to others that we ourselves have received. Forgiving others is essential, as we have already covered. We forgive those who have wounded us, hurt us. This act of forgiveness frees us and puts the other person in God's hands. Jesus knew that to keep our peace of mind, forgiveness is a must!

And lead us not into temptation, But deliver us from the evil one.

Jesus teaches us to ask God for His help in avoiding temptation. I think it's interesting how Jesus puts temptation and the evil one in the same sentence. Jesus knows that the devil comes to tempt us. Referring back to chapter 2 on the principle of agreement, the devil comes to tempt us to agree with him. Jesus taught us to ask God to deliver us from the schemes of the devil. It's in our prayer time that we ask God to give us the strength to resist the devil throughout our day.

For Yours [God's] is the kingdom and the power and the glory forever. Amen

Jesus ends this prayer with further praise of the power and glory of God. Jesus taught us to end our prayer with the acknowledgement of who God is.

Jesus gave us this prayer to teach us how to pray. I don't say every detail of this prayer every day, but I do pray most parts of this prayer each day. We don't want to become ritualistic and mumble words that have lost their meaning. It's important to worship God and tell Him our needs and concerns in our own words. In our own words we need to ask Him to forgive us when we have made a mistake. In our own words we need to talk to Him when someone has hurt or betrayed us. In our own words we need to ask for His help in forgiving others. In our own words we need to remind the devil that we belong to God and that God protects us.

DESPERATE TIMES

I have described above a solid foundation of prayer and communication with God. That solid foundation is like our meat and potatoes that our soul and spirit need to grow. However, there are times when our soul and spirit needs a B12 shot. I would be amiss if I did not share with you what prayer can look like in desperate situations. There are times when we come to God and we are exhausted from the emotional or physical battle. In times like this I will begin to say the name of *Jesus, Jesus, Jesus*! Through tears and a heavy heart I cry out to Him and pour out the anguish in my soul. I will say to God, *"Help!* I am out of strategies and strength."

There is a song that I am going to encourage you to look up and listen to "Lord, I Need You" by Matt Maher. You can Google it to find it in several places. This song is three minutes long. As you listen to the entire song you can feel the anguish in your heart leave as you pray and say these words in the song back to God.

LORD, I NEED YOU

Lord, I come, I confess
Bowing here, I find my rest
Without You, I fall apart
You're the One that guides my heart

Lord, I need You, oh, I need You
Every hour I need You
My one defense, my righteousness
Oh, God, how I need You

Where sin runs deep, Your grace is more
Where grace is found, is where You are
Where You are, Lord I am free
Holiness is Christ in me

Lord, I need You, oh, I need You
Every hour I need You
My one defense, my righteousness
Oh, God, how I need You

Teach my song to rise to you
When temptation comes my way,
When I cannot stand I'll fall on You
Jesus, You're my hope and stay

Lord, I need You, oh, I need You
Every hour I need You
My one defense, my righteousness
Oh, God, how I need You

You're my one defense, my righteousness
Oh, God how I need You
My one defense, my righteousness
Oh, God, how I need You

Just like this song says, there are times when our soul is simply crying out, "Oh, God, how I need You." Pouring our soul to God is also an effective way to pray. We find king David did this often in the psalms. David becomes vulnerable and humble before God as he petitions Him with the sorrows of his heart. God refers to David as, "A man after My own heart" (Acts 13:22). There are times when falling on our knees and telling God we need Him every minute of our day is also important.

In the closing of this chapter, it's important to understand that having a relationship with God makes all the difference in our lives. God is pleased when we seek Him out. He says, "Call to Me, and I will answer you, and show you great and mighty things, which you do not know" (Jer. 33:3). He knows us best and He knows best how to repair our lives. What is your relationship with God like? Have you been living for Him for years but want to grow deeper in your relationship? Or, are you new in your friendship with God and not sure how to get started? Either way, below are two prayers to help you get to know Him more. The first is a prayer to begin a relationship with God. The second prayer is to grow in greater depths in your relationship with God. As you seek God He will reveal Himself to you.

Prayer *to Begin* a Relationship with God

God, I believe that because of Your great love for me You sent Jesus to rescue me from my past shortcomings and sins. I am tired of trying to figure out how to live my life without Your help. I confess that Jesus is the Lord and Savior of my life. I surrender my heart to You and ask for Your wisdom and guidance. I ask that Your Holy Spirit would reveal to me Your great affection and compassion for me. I thank You for opening my spiritual eyes to learn Your truths and Your ways. In Jesus' name I pray. Amen.

Prayer *to Grow* in Greater Depths with God

God, I believe that You are my Rescuer, my Savior, and my Healer; but I desire to know You more. Remove the hindrances from my life that have kept me from knowing You intimately. Just like David I say to You, "As the deer pants for the water brooks, So pants my soul for You, O God." I want to experience Your presence like I never have before. Help me to read Your word with greater passion and zeal. Holy Spirit, I hunger and thirst for more of You. Lead me into greater levels of Your presence and power. In Jesus' name I pray. Amen.

Chapter 13

A New Door

There is a door open for us. This door will take us from living in negativity to living a better quality of life. It all starts with our thoughts. If we go through the process of learning to resist the negative thoughts and *make the decision* to focus on scripture, then anything is possible! As we change what we mediate upon, doors of promise and opportunity can begin to open.

God's Open Doors

God is all powerful and He can perform miracles in our life. I have experienced both great and small miracles from God. I have treasured and thanked Him for both. God desires to do both great and small miracles in your life. This is God's nature. When the doors are opened by the hand of God, we need to walk through them.

It's important to know that *because of* the challenges we have faced, new doors can open for us. It is *because of* the hardships that we have faced that we are better equipped to move forward. The Bible teaches us that we go *from* trouble *to* hope and expectation.

From Trouble to Hope

> And I will speak tenderly and to her heart. There I will give her, her vineyards and make the Valley of Achor [troubling] to be for her *a door of hope and expectation*. And she shall sing there and respond as in the days of her youth and as at the time when she came up out of the land of Egypt. And it shall be in that day, says the Lord, that you will call me Ishi [my Husband], and you shall no more call Me Baali [my Baal].
> —Hosea 2:14–16, amp, emphasis added

I want to focus on when God says, "The Valley of Achor [the valley of her trouble] will be for her *a door of hope and expectation.*" When we have experienced times of great troubles in our life, there is a promise that our troubles can lead to a "door of hope and expectation."

You might say, "How is it possible that my troubles can lead to a *door* of hope and expectation?" I want to create a word picture to explain this. Picture a large swimming pool with a dangerously tall diving board on it. We are standing on that tall diving board looking down on the water. We are afraid and alone standing on that diving board. The sun is painfully hot and we are exhausted from the heat and negative thoughts that are bombarding our minds. Others and life circumstances have forced us up on this dangerously high diving board. We don't want to be there. When we were climbing the steep steps to the diving board we didn't realize each step was taking us to a place we didn't want to be. We can't go back down the steps because at the bottom of the steps are the same circumstances that led us to climb the diving board. We know we can't go backwards and we are afraid to move forward. The "door" that is opened for us is that crystal blue water twenty feet below. We didn't value the water when we are on the sidewalk of the pool with no fears to think about. But from this perspective we now understand the water is exactly what we need. The water that we are contemplating *jumping* into represents for us safety from the heat, peace from anxiety, and refreshment for our weary soul. The water represents the Holy Spirit. As soon as we decide to jump in the water (walk through the door) the Holy Spirit is there waiting with healing and hope.

Jesus promised us, that He would send us "the Helper, the Holy Spirit" (John 14:26), who is also our Comforter, Counselor, Intercessor, Strengthener, and Teacher. He will guide us through this life and even into the life to come—heaven.

The Holy Spirit is there waiting for us to jump, waiting for us to walk through the door. The Holy Spirit longs for us to rest in Him. The Holy Spirit is waiting for us to seek out His counsel and His power. The troubles we have experienced are a springboard to help others and a springboard to fulfill God's plan for our lives. The Bible teaches us that the same Spirit, *the Holy Spirit*, who raised Christ from the dead lives in you (Rom. 8:11). If you have surrendered your heart to Jesus, this promise is for you.

You see, much like the refreshing swimming pool, the Holy Spirit longs to be our refreshment from the strongholds that have been choking us. There are many who have come before us who have survived their troubles and impacted their world through the help of the Holy Spirit.

What New Things Are Behind That Door?

The door of hope and expectation is there *because of* the troubles you have faced. It is *because of* your trials and troubles that God is building new muscles you didn't know you had. It is *because of* those troubles that you have a new character and a new heart. Begin to get excited that you are in the process of changing and growing.

Those negative patterns of thought are going to be more easily recognizable and less of a stronghold in your life. There has been a purpose in your pain. If it

A New Door

were not for your difficulties you may not have seen that door of hope and expectation. Better days are in store for you and your family!

The apostle John recounts the vision he had of the throne room of heaven. He begins by saying, "I looked, and behold, a door standing open in heaven. And the first voice which I heard was like a trumpet speaking with me" (Rev. 4:1).

God has open doors that He wants to reveal to you. As you spend time with Him and listen for His voice, He will show you His specific plan for your life. Some of us have been living in a house filled with negativity and problem after problem; but I say to you that God has open doors for you. Not only is He delivering you from the old house of negativity but He is opening new doors of peace of mind, liking who you are, forgiving others, and a healed heart. There are doors of opportunities, doors to achieve your heart's desires, doors to live out your dreams. There is nothing negative about God!

FROM THE OLD TO THE NEW

Door in the scriptures represents an opening or entrance. It represents an opportunity to do something new. This concept of transitioning from the old and the negative to the new is not my opinion, but it comes from the words of God. The scriptures below teach us about the transition from the old to the new. The scriptures below reveal to us the very heart of God.

> I will make you inhabited as in former times, and *do better for you than at your beginnings*. Then you shall know that I am the Lord.
> —Ezekiel 36:11, emphasis added

> You [God] have turned for me my mourning into dancing.
> —Psalm 30:11

> "The glory of this latter temple [our dwelling, our household] shall be greater than the former," says the Lord of hosts. "And in this place I will give peace," says the Lord of hosts.
> —Haggai 2:9

> I will perform that good thing which I have promised to the house of Israel [your house].
> —Jeremiah 33:14

Joseph says to his brothers:

> But as for you, you meant evil against me; but God meant it for good, in order to bring it about as it is this day, to save many people alive.
> —Genesis 50:20

> So the Lord blessed the latter days of Job more than his beginning.
> —Job 42:12

God promises us that our future is going to be better than our past *when we turn to Him*. This is good news. We see this in the lives of many in the Bible, and we see this in countless testimonies of people whom God has restored. There are many people in the Bible whose struggles turned around for the better as the scriptures above teach; but there is one person from the Bible I want to focus on, and that person is Job. I have already addressed some of Job's issues in the beginning of the book, but his life is a lesson in the tender care of God restoring us. Everything that could go wrong for Job did. But in the end everything that could go *right* for Job did.

JOB

Most of us know the story of Job. The Bible calls Job a "blameless and upright man, one who feared God and shunned evil" (Job 1:1). God was actually bragging on Job by calling him a blameless man. The Bible tells us there was no one else like him on the earth. In Job 1:10 we read where Satan tells God that Job is a good man only because God has prospered him and "blessed the work of his hands." In the next verse Satan challenges God to remove the hedge of protection from Job and remove His blessing from his life. If You do this, Satan tells God, Job "will surely curse You to Your face!" (v. 11).

God had confidence in Job, and God tells the devil that he may take all that Job has, only he must not take his life (v. 12). As we follow Job in verses 13–19, he soon got news that his children were killed and all his possessions were gone. Job still would not curse God (v. 22). Then Satan attacked Job's health, and Job was covered "with painful boils from the sole of his feet to the crown of his head" (2:7). After all of this Job's wife said to him, just "curse God and die!" (v. 9). But Job still would not sin against God (v. 10). Job lost his children, his health, and his fortune. The Bible tells us Job's "grief was very great" (v. 13). The Greek word translated *grief* in this verse means mental and physical pain, sorrow, and sadness.

Through all of his afflictions, Job never cursed God. He did, however, despise his very existence by cursing the day he was born (3:1). This shows us that Job experienced some of the toxic thinking that you and I experience. Job's circumstances probably trump what we have gone through. I am not going to outline all the details of Job's life, expect to say from chapter 3 to chapter 42 God took Job through a healing process—a process of removing wrong thoughts about himself and wrong thoughts about God; a process of forgiving his friends and repenting for wrong mindsets. In fact, by the time we get to the end of the Book of Job, it's as though he has walked through a new door in his thoughts and perspectives. When we fast-forward to the end of this difficult season of his life, Job says,

> Then Job answered the LORD and said: "I know that You can do everything, And that no purpose of Yours can be withheld from You. You asked, 'Who is this who hides counsel without knowledge?' Therefore I have uttered what I did not understand, Things too wonderful for me, which I did not know. Listen, please, and let me speak; You said, 'I will question you, and you shall answer Me.' I have heard of You by the hearing of the ear, But now *my eye sees You*. Therefore I abhor myself, And repent in dust and ashes."
> —JOB 42:1–6

God was not the author of Job's problems, but by the end of this trial Job had a clearer perspective of who God was and who he (Job) was not. He repented for his wrong mindsets and was able to see God more clearly.

We learn in Job 42 that God restored to Job double for all that he lost in this difficult season. One of my most cherished verses in the Bible is found in Job 42:12.

> Now the LORD blessed the latter days of Job more than his beginning;...After this Job lived one hundred and forty years, and saw his children and grandchildren for four generations. So Job died, old and full of days.
> —JOB 42:12, 16–17

God blessed the remainder of Job's days. When the text says that God *blessed* his latter days, this means God granted Job favor and contentment. Even the New Testament speaks of Job's trial and the outcome of his difficult season,

> Indeed we count them blessed who endure. You have heard of the perseverance of Job and seen the end intended by the Lord—that the Lord is very compassionate and merciful.
> —JAMES 5:11

Job stayed faithful to God and God blessed Job *double* for all his grief, sorrow, and pain. In Isaiah 61:7 it says, "Therefore in their land they shall posses double." This teaches us that if we just hang in there and faint not (Gal. 6:9, KJV), we too will see God restore double to us. The Book of James says it best when it says we have seen the perseverance of Job and the end intended by the Lord. It was Job's perseverance that led to his good outcome. Job lived a long, healthy, blessed life, "full of days," seeing up to four generations. God in His miracle working power was able to restore Job. The same will be true for us if don't quit. Let us persevere like Job, and wait to see God transition us from the former to the latter.

Your Next Chapter

God desires to take you from the valley of trouble to the door of hope. He promises to make our future greater than our past. It is the very troubles that we have experienced that can open the door to a new beginning.

There are a few questions I want to ask you below that can bring revelation as to how God might turn your tragedy into your triumph. Take a few moments in your quiet time with God to contemplate the thoughts below.

I ask you,

- What are you qualified for *because of* your trouble?
- What new purpose or assignments does God want to give to you *because* you walked through such difficulties?
- How can you better relate to others and help them in their time of need *because of* your own pain?
- What new things has God got in store for you *because of* your trouble?

Even if you're not ready to go out tomorrow and bring what you've learned to the world, I would suggest to you *start dreaming*. Begin to discover how the Holy Spirit desires to turn your past into some else's victory. Begin to get a vision for your life and write it down.

I remember recently I was speaking at a women's breakfast and the presence of the Holy Spirit was very strong in the room. And I remember thinking, "I feel qualified to address these women today because of all the hell that I went through." I recognized in that moment that I'm still standing and more confident in God then I have ever been!

God has the same intention for you. Begin to talk to God and those you trust about how you can help someone else. Or, how you can begin an endeavor that would help others? Begin to seek God on how to accomplish your God-given assignment. You were put on this earth for more than merely surviving life's hardships. You were put on this earth for more than just existing. You were put on this earth to fulfill your God-given dreams!

Just like that scripture says, "There I will give back her vineyards to her and transform her Valley of Troubles into a Door of Hope. She will respond to me there, singing with joy" (Hosea 2:15, TLB). As I look back, I am thankful for the difficult seasons of life that I have gone through, because without those difficulties I would not be the person I am today. And I like the person I am today. I would not have learned many invaluable lessons that can only be learned by letting God heal my heart. I have watched God lead me out of trouble and into a good place. I love God all the more because He has been my way maker, my comfort, my strong tower, and my defense. He has become my best friend and someone I can count on in the storms of life. It is *because of* my "troubles" that I have great hope and expectation from God. I am swimming in that pool where the Holy Spirit dwells waiting to see the good that God desires to bring to my front door. As you walk through the door there is magnificent hope and expectation waiting for you!

It's time to seek God on what your next chapter is? It's time to ask the Holy Spirit how you can be His heart and hands in this world. Below I have a prayer to begin the process of asking God what is on the other side of that door for you.

PRAYER

God, I thank You that there has been a purpose in my pain. I know that You are not the author of the evil that has happened in my life but You are the Author of my healing and restoration. God, I lay down my agenda for my life and I ask You to show me Your assignment for my life. I confess that I need Your help and the wisdom of the Holy Spirit. Please bring the right people and resources into my life to help me accomplish Your will. Help me to not get discouraged when the process is taking longer than I expect, and give me signs along the way that I am moving in the right direction. If there are any wrong mindsets or relationships that need to go in my life, help me to let them go. I trust that You are going to do exceedingly abundantly above all that I could ask or think (Eph. 3:20). I wait expectantly and excitedly for You. In Jesus' name I pray, amen.

Chapter 14

COLLECTION OF PRAYERS

I WANT TO THANK you for all the soul searching and praying you have done throughout this book. It has been my prayer that what has been discussed will be a catalyst for change in your life. As the title of the third section of this book says, we are all in a process of "continuing to overcome." At times life confronts us with anger, worry, stress, fear, depression, guilt, rejection, or unforgiveness. When these issues arise I would encourage you to go back and refer to the chapter on the emotion you are facing. Sometimes we forget nuggets of wisdom that can help us to overcome. When I am confronted with these types of emotions, I have to put into practice what I have discussed in this book. The expectation *is not* that you will never experience any of these negative emotions; the goal is that they will not build strongholds in your life.

THE PURPOSE OF THIS CHAPTER

I have designed this chapter to be a compilation of all of the prayers that were listed at the end of each chapter. There may be times when you need to go back and reread an individual chapter, or there may also be times when you just want the prayer pertaining to the negative emotion. I have listed below each prayer from each chapter. I am confident that the Holy Spirit will lead you as you walk toward victory over negative emotions. This is not the end of a book, but the beginning of a new way to keep free from long-term emotional wounds.

I would encourage you to say the prayers below out loud. They are more effective when your brain hears what comes out of your mouth.

HEALING PRAYER (CHAPTER 1)

God, I ask for Your wisdom, strength, and comfort as I begin this process of healing my damaged emotions. Holy Spirit, I look to You for guidance in this process. Help me to be willing and patient to look at and examine any destructive emotional roots that need to be removed. I thank You that Your desire is for me to be whole and healthy. I put my hand in Yours now and begin this process. In Jesus name I pray. Amen.

Agreement Prayer (Chapter 2)

Lord, I pray the same prayer the psalmist prayed: "Search me, O God, and know my heart; test me and know my anxious thoughts. See if there is any offensive way in me, and lead me in the way everlasting" (Psalm 139:23-24, NIV). You have written Your desires for me on my heart. Help me not to be tempted with fears that ensnare my thoughts, my heart, and my actions. These agreements bring on grief and sinfulness. God, I repent for my wrongful agreements with Satan. I thank You that I am released from these agreements. I thank You for promising to be with me, to be my strength in times of trouble and in times of temptation. Bring me into agreement with Your perfect will and plan for my life. In Jesus name I pray. Amen.

Breaker Declaration (Chapter 3)

I here and now reject and disown all the sins of my ancestors. As one who has been delivered from the power of darkness and translated into the kingdom of God's dear Son, I cancel out all demonic working that may have been passed on to me from my ancestors. As one who has been crucified and raised with Jesus Christ and who sits with Him in heavenly places, I renounce all satanic assignments that are directed toward me and my ministry, and I cancel every curse that Satan and his workers have put on me. I announce to Satan and all his forces that Christ became a curse for me (Gal. 3:13) when He died for my sins on the cross. I reject any and every way in which Satan may ownership of me. I belong to the Lord Jesus Christ, who purchased me with His own blood. I reject all other blood sacrifices whereby Satan may claim ownership of me. I declare myself to be eternally and completely signed over and committed to the Lord Jesus Christ. By the authority that I have in Christ Jesus, I now command every familiar spirit and every enemy of the Lord Jesus Christ to leave my presence. I commit myself to my heavenly Father to do His will from this day forward. In Jesus' name I pray. Amen.[1]

Stress Prayer (Chapter 4)

Heavenly Father, I ask You to help me get to the source of my stress. As I begin this journey of healing from negative thinking, show me the stumbling blocks that have kept me bound. Give me the strength to go from the surface issue to the root of the issue. Grant me the wisdom to know which remedy

I need to overcome a stressful situation. God, I also seek Your grace to heal my mind, body, and spirit. I look to You, Holy Spirit, for Your counsel as I begin this process of restoration. Thank You in advance for the good things that You have in my future. In Jesus' name I pray. Amen.

Broken Heart Prayer (Chapter 5)

God, You see the hurts buried deep in my heart. Father, give me the courage to face and grieve over the emotional pain I have been carrying. Holy Spirit, I ask You to be with me as I allow myself to examine painful areas from my past, and I ask You to show me any roots that need to be removed from my heart. I make a decision to put my heartbreaks on your alter and not to pick them up again. Help me to lend forgiveness to others so I can move forward in freedom. I desire to be free of a heavy heart, and I want to be able to love others without bringing baggage from my past into my current relationships. I'm tired of living my life from a place of pain, and I am ready for the healing process to begin. Lord, I look to You to bring me step-by-step into liberty and to bring healing to my body, soul, and spirit. I pray, Holy Spirit, that You would supernaturally restore my physical body as my soul begins to heal (3 John 1:2). In Jesus' name I pray. Amen.

Self-Reproach Prayer (Chapter 6)

God, I pray You would help me to recognize when rejection tries to steal my peace and rob my identity that is found in You. Continue to teach me how to use Your Word to defeat the lies of rejection. Help me to see that I am worthwhile and valuable in Your eyes. I accept the truth that I don't need the approval of others to like who I am. I stand not in my own righteousness but in the righteousness of Jesus Christ. Holy Spirit, wrap me in the truth that I am loved and cherished by You. Grant me the grace to love myself, including my strengths and weaknesses. I will meditate on Your love letter to me, the Bible. In Jesus' name I pray. Amen.

Guilt and Accusation Prayer (Chapter 7)

Jesus, I come to You with this burden of guilt. I am tired and exhausted from the weight of guilt and shame. I no longer desire to walk with the embarrassment and shame from my mistakes. I ask You to give me the strength and the wisdom to trade my guilty past for Your great love for me.

Holy Spirit, I ask You to show me if guilt and accusation tries to reenter my life. Help me to know that through Your death and resurrection, You nailed my sin, shame, and guilt to the cross. I accept Your redemption and I accept Your restoration in my life. I thank You that my past guilt no longer has a foothold in my life and I can be free to heal—body, soul, and spirit. I now understand that Your cross is enough to cover my mistakes. I thank You that You love me and desire for me to walk in physical, emotional, and spiritual health. In Jesus' name I pray. Amen.

Worry, Anxiety, and Fear Prayer (Chapter 8)

Holy Spirit, I ask You to reveal the known and unknown roots behind my fear. I am tired from this tormenting spirit of fear, and I look to You to show me the way out of fear. I understand that I have felt a lack of love in my life and I can now rest securely in Your love and protection. I confess my agreement with the spirit of fear, and I pray You would show me how to shut the door to the devil's foothold of fear in my life. I pray You would supernaturally reverse the negative effects that fear has had on my mind and my body. In faith, I thank You for showing me how to walk in godly peace. In Jesus' name I pray. Amen.

Depression Prayer (Chapter 9)

God, I come to You tired of this battle with depression. Please give me the wisdom to know when my thoughts are producing the emotional and physical response of despair. I break all ties, alignments, and agreements that I have made with negative thinking concerning my life, my future, and my family. Holy Spirit, grant me the grace to see the good that You have in store for my life. I ask You, God, to bring times of refreshing and restoration to my life. In Jesus' name I pray. Amen.

Anger and Bitterness Prayer (Chapter 10)

God, I want to be free from all anger and bitterness. I no longer want to give place to the anger and bitterness in my heart. I release to You all the people (and at times even You) who I have been angry and bitter with. I want to be cleansed of the offenses that I have carried in the deep recesses of my heart. I ask You to forgive me for my anger and bitterness. And forgive me for thinking I needed to see justice before I could forgive. I now look forward to the fresh start and new beginnings that You have planned for my future. In Jesus' name I pray. Amen.

UNFORGIVENESS PRAYER (CHAPTER 11)

Prayer to forgive someone else

Dear heavenly Father, You see the wound in my heart this person has caused me. You know all the reasons behind their actions. Today I make the choice to forgive them. God, I release this person into Your hands. I will not seek revenge upon them for their actions but I pray Your mercy in their life. I pray You would cleanse and restore my mind, my body, and my spirit from their offense. Thank You that You have heard my prayer and that You are faithful to restore my joy and peace back to me. In Jesus' name I pray. Amen.

Prayer to forgive yourself

God, I admit my wrongdoing and my mistake, I shouldn't have done what I did. I'm going to lay my sin at Your cross. I am going to learn from this experience and accept the forgiveness that You desire to give to me. Jesus, I thank You that Your blood will cover my sin and my shame. God, if I have caused anyone pain or hurt, I pray that Your Holy Spirit will minster life and peace to that person or that situation. God, I accept Your mercy and forgiveness and I now choose to forgive myself. Once again, I now choose to forgive myself. I no longer will see myself or get my identity from my mistakes. I thank You for the new beginnings You have in store for my life. In Jesus' name I pray. Amen.

YOUR RELATIONSHIP WITH GOD PRAYER (CHAPTER 12)

Prayer to begin a relationship with God

God, I believe that because of Your great love for me You sent Jesus to rescue me from my past shortcomings and sins. I am tired of trying to figure out how to live my life without Your help. I confess that Jesus is the Lord and Savior of my life. I surrender my heart to You and ask for Your wisdom and guidance. I ask that Your Holy Spirit would reveal to me Your great affection and compassion for me. I thank You for opening my spiritual eyes to learn Your truths and Your ways. In Jesus' name I pray. Amen.

Prayer to *grow in* greater depths with God

God, I believe that You are my Rescuer, my Savior, and my Healer; but I desire to know You more. Remove the hindrances from my life that have kept me from knowing You intimately. Just like David I say to You, "As the deer pants for the water brooks, So pants my soul for You, O God" (Ps. 42:1). I want to experience Your presence like I never have before. Help me to read Your word with greater passion and zeal. Holy Spirit, I hunger and thirst for more of You. Lead me into greater levels of Your presence and power. In Jesus' name I pray. Amen.

A NEW DOOR PRAYER (CHAPTER 13)

God, I thank You that there has been a purpose in my pain. I know that You are not the author of the evil that has happened in my life but You are the Author of my healing and restoration. God, I lay down my agenda for my life and I ask You to show me Your assignment for my life. I confess that I need Your help and the wisdom of the Holy Spirit. Please bring the right people and resources into my life to help me accomplish Your will. Help me to not get discouraged when the process is taking longer than I expect, and give me signs along the way that I am moving in the right direction. If there are any wrong mindsets or relationships that need to go in my life, help me to let them go. I trust that You are going to do exceedingly abundantly above all that I could ask or think (Eph. 3:20). I wait expectantly and excitedly for You. In Jesus' name I pray, amen.

Notes

Introduction

1. Joseph Mercola, "Stress Linked to Cancer," Dr. Mercola's Comments, *Mercola.com*, http://articles.mercola.com/sites/articles/archive/2010/02/04/stress-linked-to-cancer.aspx (accessed September 13, 2014).

Chapter 1
When Nothing Is Working

1. Mercola.
2. Ibid.
3. Ibid.
4. Ibid.
5. "About Dr. Mercola," *Joseph Mercola*, http://www.mercola.com/forms/background.htm (accessed September 17, 2014).
6. "About Bruce Lipton," *Mountain of Love Productions*, https://www.brucelipton.com/about (accessed September 17, 2014).
7. Bruce Lipton, "The Biology of Belief: Unleashing the Power of Consciousness, Matter & Miracles," *Mountain of Love Productions*, https://www.brucelipton.com/books/biology-of-belief (accessed September 13, 2014).
8. Anando, "It's Now a Proven Fact—Your Unconscious Mind Is Running Your Life," *Lifetrainings.com*, http://www.lifetrainings.com/Your-unconscious-mind-is-running-you-life.html (accessed September 13, 2014).
9. Robert M. Sargis, "An Overview of the Hypothalamus," updated June 10, 2014, Endocrineweb, *Vertical Health*, http://www.endocrineweb.com/endocrinology/overview-hypothalamus (accessed September 13, 2014).

Chapter 3
Origin of Negative Thought

1. "The Jukes Family," *Wikipedia*, updated May 6, 2014, http://en.wikipedia.org/wiki/The_Jukes_family (accessed September 14, 2014).
2. "Richard Louis Dugdale," *Wikipedia*, updated March 26, 2014, http://en.wikipedia.org/wiki/Richard_L._Dugdale (accessed September 14, 2014).
3. Al Sanders, *Crisis in Morality* (Los Angeles: Bible Institute of Los Angeles, 195?), quoted in Leonard Ravenhill, "Jonathan Edwards," *Dayspring*, 1963, Bethany House Publishers, *Ravenhill.org*, http://www.ravenhill.org/edwards.htm (accessed September 13, 2014).
4. Neil Anderson, *The Bondage Breaker* (Eugene, OR: Harvest House, 1990).

Chapter 4
Stress

1. "Hans Selye's General Adaptation Syndrome," *The Essence of Stress Relief*, http://www.essenceofstressrelief.com/general-adaptation-syndrome.html (accessed September 13, 2014).

2. "General Adaptation Syndrome: Stress a Useful Reaction?" *Gale Encyclopedia of Medicine*, The Gale Group, http://medical-dictionary.thefreedictionary.com/general+adaptation+syndrome (accessed September 13, 2014).

3. Ibid.

4. "Hans Selye's General Adaptation Syndrome."

5. Ibid.

6. Ibid.

7. Neil Neimark, "5 Minute Stress Mastery," *5minuestressmastery.com*, http://www.thebodysoulconnection.com/EducationCenter/fight.html (accessed September 19, 2014).

8. "How to Identify and Cope with Your PTSD," About Health, *About.com*, http://ptsd.about.com/od/selfhelp/a/CopingTriggers.htm (accessed September 19, 2014).

9. "Hans Selye's General Adaptation Syndrome."

10. "Resistance Stage," Stress, Health & Life, *Google Sites*, https://sites.google.com/site/stresshealthandlife/stress-response/2---resistant-stage (accessed September 19, 2014).

11. "Hans Selye's General Adaptation Syndrome."

12. George Chrousos, "Stress and Disorders of the Stress System," "Concepts of Homeostasis and Stress," *Medscape*, http://www.medscape.com/viewarticle/704866_2 (accessed September 19, 2014).

13. "Effect of Stress on the Brain," *HowStuffWorks*, http://health.howstuffworks.com/wellness/stress-management/effect-of-stress-on-the-brain.htm (accessed September 19, 2014).

14. "50 Common Signs and Symptoms," *The American Institute of Stress*, http://www.stress.org/stress-effects/ (accessed September 19, 2014).

15. "Exhaustion Stage," Stress, Health & Life, *Google Sites*, https://sites.google.com/site/stresshealthandlife/stress-response/3---exhaustion-stage (accessed September 19, 2014).

16. Ibid.

17. Ibid.

18. Ibid.

19. Jacob Teitelbaum, "Is Stress Exhausting Your Adrenal System," *The Oz Show* (blog), February 4, 2010, http://www.doctoroz.com/blog/jacob-teitelbaum-md/stress-exhausting-your-adrenal-system (accessed September 18, 2014).

20. Michael Smith, "Immune system Busters & Boosters," October 24, 2013, Cold, Flu, & Cough Health Center, *WebMD*, http://www.webmd.com/cold-and-flu/10-immune-system-busters-boosters (accessed September 18, 2014).

21. David Abbott, "Zero Tolerance to Negative Thinking," *Maxing Out Media*, http://zerotolerancetonegativethinking.com/Positive%20thinking%20creates%20a%20positive%20brain.htm (accessed September 18, 2014).

Notes   171

22. "Exercising to Relax," Harvard Health Publications, *Harvard Medical School*, http://www.health.harvard.edu/newsletters/Harvard_Mens_Health_Watch/2011/February/exercising-to-relax (accessed September 18, 2014).

CHAPTER 5
BROKEN HEART

1. "Diseases and Conditions: Broken Heart Syndrome," *Mayo Foundation for Medical Education and Research*, http://www.mayoclinic.org/diseases-conditions/broken-heart-syndrome/basics/definition/con-20034635 (accessed September 13, 2014).

2. Kathleen Fackelmann, "'Broken-heart syndrome' Has Medical Link," *USA Today*, February 9, 2005, http://usatoday30.usatoday.com/news/health/2005-02-09-broken-hearts_x.htm (accessed September 13, 2014).

3. Dulce Zamora, "Death from a Broken Heart," *WebMD*, November 24, 2003, *MedicineNet*, Inc, http://archive.today/csfaH (accessed September 13, 2014).

4. American Physiological Society, "Anticipating a Laugh Reduces Our Stress Hormones, Study Shows," *Science Daily*, http://www.sciencedaily.com/releases/2008/04/080407114617.htm (accessed September 14, 2014).

5. "Humor Therapy," *Larry Hartwig Joyful Aging*, http://www.joyfulaging.com/HumorTherapy.htm (accessed September 14, 2014).

6. "Introduction to Hematology," *Puget Sound Blood Center*, http://www.psbc.org/hematology/02_how.htm (accessed September 19, 2014).

7. Tim Taylor, "Immune and Lymphatic Systems," InnerBody, *HowtoMedia, Inc*, http://www.innerbody.com/image/lympov.html (accessed September 14, 2014).

CHAPTER 6
SELF-REPROACH

1. Sargis.

CHAPTER 7
GUILT AND ACCUSATION

1. Dale Fletcher, "Sin, Guilt and Your Health—A Health Devotional. Psalm 32:1–6," Faith and Health Connection, *Peterson Media Group*, http://www.faithandhealthconnection.org/sin-guilt-and-health-psalm-321-6-health-devotional/ (accessed September 14, 2014).

2. "Blood Test: Immunoglobulins…," *About Kids Health*, http://kidshealth.org/parent/system/medical/test_immunoglobulins.html (accessed September 20, 2014).

CHAPTER 8
WORRY, ANXIETY, AND FEAR

1. Caroline Leaf, "Controlling Your Toxic Thoughts," *Dr. Caroline Leaf*, http://drleaf.com/about/toxic-thoughts/ (accessed September 16, 2014).

2. Stin Hansen, "Metaphysics for Your Mind," *Mythoughtcoach.com*, http://mythoughtcoach.com/Why.aspx (accessed September 21, 2014).

3. Ibid.

4. Donald Colbert, interview, *getv.org* (January 18, 2013), John Hagee Ministries, San Antonio, Texas.

5. John Maxwell, *Thinking for a Change* (New York: Warner, 2003).

6. Smith Wigglesworth quote in J.J. DiPietro, "Smith Wigglesworth," What Is Your Legacy, Cane Creek Church, http://www.canecreekchurch.org/what-s-your-legacy/44-smith-wigglesworth (accessed September 21, 2014).

7. "Hans Selye's General Adaptation Syndrome."

8. Chrousos.

9. Mayo Clinic Staff, "Agoraphobia," Diseases and Conditions, *Mayo Foundation for Medical Education and Research*, http://www.mayoclinic.org/diseases-conditions/agoraphobia/basics/definition/con-20029996 (accessed September 21, 2014).

10. David Carbonell, "What Causes Panic Attacks," *Anxiety Coach*, http://www.anxietycoach.com/causes-panic-attacks.html (accessed September 21, 2014).

11. Henry Wright quote in Cathy DeMar, "Faith or Fear," August 5, 2013, *Liberty House Ministry* (blog)http://www.libertyhouseministry.com/2013/08/faith-or-fear.html (accessed September 21, 2014).

12. Mercola.

CHAPTER 9
DEPRESSION

1. R.V. Parsey et al., "Lower Serotonin Transporter Binding Potential in the Human Brain During Major Depressive Episodes," American Journal of Psychiatry 163, no. 1(January 2006): 52–58, http://www.ncbi.nlm.nih.gov/pubmed/16390889 (accessed September 22, 2014).

2. Joseph Goldberg, "Causes of Depression," *WebMD*, February 8, 2014, http://www.webmd.com/depression/guide/causes-depression (accessed September 15, 2014).

3. Regina Bailey, "Amygdala," *About.com*, http://biology.about.com/od/anatomy/p/Amygdala.htm (accessed September 15, 2014).

4. "Diseases and Conditions: Depression (Major Depression)," *Mayo Foundation for Medical Education and Research*, http://www.mayoclinic.org/diseases-conditions/depression/basics/causes/con-20032977 (accessed September 15, 2014).

5. "What Causes Depression?" Harvard Health Publications, *Harvard Medical School*, http://www.health.harvard.edu/newsweek/what-causes-depression.htm (accessed September 15, 2014).

6. Joseph M. Carver, "Emotional Memory Management: Positive Control over Your Memory," found at New Hope Outreach, "Thoughts Change Brain Chemistry," *Wordpress*, http://newhopeoutreach.wordpress.com/related-articles/recovery-from-abuse/healing-emotional-memories/thoughts-change-brain-chemistry/ (accessed September 14, 2014).

7. Joseph M. Carver, "Emotional Memory Management: Positive Control over Your Memory," found at New Hope Outreach, "The Brain Doesn't Care Which File Is Active," *Wordpress*, http://newhopeoutreach.wordpress.com/related-articles/recovery-from-abuse/healing-emotional-memories/the-brain-doesnt-care-which-file-is-active-2/ (accessed September 14, 2014).

8. Jo-Anne Puggioni, "How I Overcame Depression—In a Nutshell!" *Princess Warrior* (blog), September 5, 2012, http://www.princesswarriorlessons.com/2012/09/how-i-overcame-depression-in-nutshell.html (accessed September 15, 2014).

9. Ibid.

10. Lipton.

11. John Spayde, "Upgrade Your Brain," *Health Fitness Magazine*, October 2010, http://experiencelife.com/article/upgrade-your-brain/ (accessed September 15, 2014).

12. Mary James, "Adrenal Fatigue and Stress: Could Stress Be Affecting Your Thyroid?" Women's Health Network, http://www.womenshealthnetwork.com/adrenal-fatigue-and-stress/could-stress-be-affecting-your-thyroid.aspx (accessed September 15, 2014).

13. Puggioni.

14. Ibid.

Chapter 10
Anger and Bitterness

1. "Our Guest Henry Wright," Sid Roth, It's Supernatural Television Series, http://www.sidroth.us/2014/03/13/our-guest-henry-wright/ (accessed September 17, 2014).

2. Elizabeth Cohen, "Blaming Others Can Ruin Your Health," CNN Health, August 18, 2011, *Turner Broadcasting System*, http://www.cnn.com/2011/HEALTH/08/17/bitter.resentful.ep/index.html?&hpt=hp_c2 (accessed September 15, 2014).

3. Concordia University, "Can Blaming Others Make People Sick?" *ScienceDaily*, http://www.sciencedaily.com/releases/2011/08/110809104259.htm (accessed September 15, 2014).

4. "Mind/Body Connection: How Your Emotions Affect Your Health," updated December 2010, *American Academy of Family Physicians*, http://familydoctor.org/familydoctor/en/prevention-wellness/emotional-wellbeing/mental-health/mind-body-connection-how-your-emotions-affect-your-health.html (accessed September 15, 2014).

Chapter 11
Unforgiveness

1. John Upledger, *A Brain Is Born* (Berkeley, CA: North Atlantic Books, 1996), 133.

2. Rose Sweet, "Forgiveness and Restoration," Focus on the Family, http://www.focusonthefamily.com/marriage/divorce_and_infidelity/forgiveness_and_restoration.aspx (accessed September 15, 2014).

Chapter 14
Collection of Prayers

1. Anderson.

About the Author

*L*uann Dunnuck is a dynamic conference speaker and author. She brings a message of hope and encouragement to those who are experiencing emotional or physical afflictions. She has overcome many obstacles in her own life, such as panic attacks and a debilitating illness. She desires to point others to wholeness and spiritual health. She looks for the joy in life and endeavors to bring good news to others. Luann has published three previous books that communicate God's love and redemptive power. Her message of hope and restoration has been heard on radio and TV, including *Words to Live By* from RBC Ministries, and *Crossroads Magazine*. She is happily married and has two amazing daughters.

Contact the Author

To contact Luann or get more information
on her teachings, visit her online at

www.LuannDunnuck.com

Companion Workbook

The companion workbook to *Holy Spirit Psychology* can be downloaded at www.LuannDunnuck.com for $9.99. A portion of the proceeds go to homeless and foster children in the United States.

Other Books by the Author

*T*hese books are available at www.luanndunnuck.com.

  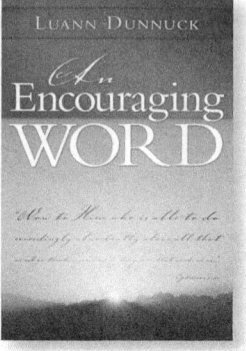

The Timeless Treasure	Chocolate, Peanut butter & Life	An Encouraging Word
978-0-9746602-0-2	978-1-59979-353-5	978-1-59185-715-0